RESHAPING THE MODERN CITY

SLCE ARCHITECTS, 1941–2018

Artifice

ESSEX
HOUSE

CONTENTS

1

INTRODUCTION

NEW YORK ARCHITECTS

BY THOMAS MELLINS

SLCE Architects is celebrating more than 75 years as one of New York's most prolific and enduring architectural firms; one with a prominent role in reshaping the NYC skyline. Its portfolio consists of more than 3,500 projects worldwide, encompassing millions of square feet. This highly respected firm works closely with both developers and not-for-profit organizations who rely on SLCE's quality and consistency in completing architectural work. In New York alone SLCE has directly participated in more development than any other architectural firm, and its projects have helped reshape every borough since its founding in 1941.

SLCE's portfolio is wide-ranging and addresses a broad variety of aesthetic, social, and economic needs. Projects include luxury condominiums, low-rise buildings, tall towers, buildings with traditional approaches and those pushing the boundaries of modernism, hospitals, hotels, religious institutions, schools, affordable housing, senior housing, single-room occupancy (SRO) housing for the formerly homeless, and renovation and rehabilitation projects. SLCE's work focuses on the art of design, the craft of building, and negotiating each project's unique challenges.

STAKING OUT TURF: FOUNDING AND EARLY GROWTH

In 1941, as New York and the nation struggled through the end of the Great Depression, two young architects—Sid Schuman and Sam Lichtenstein, who had met while working in the design department of Bell Telephone Company—decided to form their own architectural firm. Schuman and Lichtenstein, graduates of Columbia University and New York University, respectively, identified what they considered to be an overlooked and potentially lucrative business: the remodeling of single-family urban row houses into multi-family dwellings.

Centering their practice in the thriving real-estate market of New York City, the architects' reputations quickly grew, and they soon diversified their work. Schuman and Lichtenstein, along with later partners Peter Claman and Al Efron, navigated a changing economic and cultural landscape with a flexible approach to style and typology that would come to define their firm into the future. Initial projects ranged from office buildings to synagogues, from cinemas to strip malls. In the 1970s, high-rise luxury rental apartment buildings became an enduring staple of the firm's work, as did hospitals, which the firm had begun to design as early as the 1950s. At the same time, SLCE added mid-rise affordable housing and senior residences, as well as adaptive reuse and rehabilitation projects, to its output.

SECRETS TO SUCCESS: EXPERTISE AND INTERNAL STRUCTURE

Providing complete architectural and design services throughout all phases of construction, SLCE remains dedicated to adhering to program and negotiating the intricacies of a given site. The firm has long been distinguished by its

Page 8: 432 Park Avenue, New York, New York

Above, from left to right Peter Claman, Al Efron, Sid Schuman, Sam Lichtenstein

knowledge of complex urban environments and its ability to bring vast technical and regulatory expertise to bear on the execution of large-scale projects. In addition to design, the firm's services include feasibility and zoning studies, masterplanning, and full contract documents. Excelling at meeting clients' expectations and requirements by completing projects within budget and on time, the firm has produced work that reflects how things get done in competitive urban real-estate markets: SLCE provides key insights into the evolution of 20th- and 21st-century architectural practice.

Originally Schuman Lichtenstein Architects, then eventually Schuman Lichtenstein Claman Efron, SLCE adopted its current name after the retirement of Al Efron in the late 1990s. Today it has 150 employees, and offices in New York and London; London-based developers working on projects in New York introduced the firm to the UK market in 2008, ultimately leading partner James Davidson to establish an office there in 2016. Seven partners, two associate partners, and 16 associates participate in a profit-sharing program. The firm is organized, according to partner Saky Yakas, "not as a pyramid, but rather like a ziggurat," with nearly all promotion internally instituted. SLCE, as described by both its partners and employees, is like a family, accommodating and nurturing long-term relationships that grow and evolve over time. Many employees have been with the firm more than 30 years. Employees work closely with partners and often develop into leaders themselves. The firm works on individual projects in teams of up to ten people, with one of the partners in charge. "We have one organization. There is no room for egos here," notes Davidson.

For more than seven decades SLCE has prospered, riding out the inevitable vicissitudes (including five major recessions) of New York's ultimately durable real-estate market. In contrast to other New York architecture firms, SLCE has stayed remarkably resilient, with its healthcare facilities projects and low-income housing developments balancing the firm's market-rate residential and commercial work.

HARNESSING CHANGE: EVOLVING BUILDING TYPOLOGIES

When SLCE was founded—and for decades afterward—many in the design community preferred office buildings, buildings on college campuses, and airport projects over housing. When SLCE began its signature work on high-rise apartment buildings, it elevated standards, using high-quality materials, raising ceiling heights, and designing distinctive and memorable façades. SLCE always believed in "building from the inside out," emphasizing pragmatic and attractive layouts. Claman aimed to create floor plans that always "respected the user" In addition to keeping up with the changing tastes and requirements of consumers, which in turn mirrored changes in the city's own development and shifting demographics.

Following the fiscal crisis of the mid-1970s, New York's economy stabilized and neighborhoods gentrified; decaying areas became vibrant and commercially marketable. As more former suburbanites moved into the city with young families, the demand for commodious housing intensified. This new market wanted upscale design as well as extensive amenities. Innovative glass, precast concrete, and stone-clad buildings began to compete with the conventional brick façades that had proliferated in the interwar and postwar eras.

In 1997, Claman stated, "When we designed a luxury two-bedroom apartment in the 1980s, it had 1,150 to 1,250 square feet. Now we give it 1,650 square feet." The Knickerbocker at 308 East 72nd Street and the Siena at 186 East 76th Street, condominiums on Manhattan's Upper East Side, were two projects that sold out, according to Claman, because, as he told the *New York Times*, "People are looking for more space; a central foyer with entrances to the sleeping areas, the kitchen, and the dining room. Ideally, there's a library off the living room with its own bathroom, so it can be used as a guest room. Dressing alcoves are a must; his and hers bathrooms off the master. Otherwise, there'll be a divorce!"

Technological innovations, including more resilient glass, more effective and efficient air-conditioning, and faster elevators have fueled stylistic changes. As SLCE partner Mario Yao puts it, "Today residential buildings go taller, twist, and turn, in an effort to stand out. Previously, a consumer was just buying an interior. Now amenities such as health clubs and swimming pools—even an indoor basketball court—are a factor. And image is important, too."

So successful have its residential projects been, that according to The Real Deal and McGraw-Hill/Dodge Analytics, SLCE has been ranked the number-one architectural firm in both New York and the nation as a whole in the production of multi-family housing.

RELATIONSHIPS: DEVELOPERS

Within the very competitive realm of New York's real-estate industry, SLCE has a reputation for being "developers' architects." The firm has worked with many of New York's leading residential developers and development organizations, including Vincent Albanese, Alchemy, Apollo, Avalon, Hyman and Daniel Brodsky, Jeffrey Katz (Sherwood Equities), Collins, Community Builders, the DeMatteis Organizations, Dermot, Dunn Development, the Durst Organization, Bruce Eichner (Continuum), Extell, Fetner, Forest City, Friedman, Gotham, Harry Helmsley, HFZ Capital, Hines, Samuel Landau, LCOR,

Manocherian Brothers, Millennium Partners, Monadnock, Related Companies, Jack Resnick & Sons, Rockrose, Rose Associates, Roseland, Stahl, RXR, Melvin Senville, Irving and Hyman Shapiro, Millard Shroder Residential, Larry Silverstein, David and Jean Solomon, TF Cornerstone, Tishman Speyer, Toll Brothers, Trinity Financial, Trump, Vornado, WorldWide, and Donald Zucker. Some developers, such as Harry Macklowe, employed SLCE early in the firm's history and continued to hire the firm as they grew into mega-developers building mega-projects. Over time, developers have been loyal to SLCE; for example, both William Zeckendorf Sr. and his son, William Jr., have worked with the firm.

Developers and landowners daily approach SLCE partners to request an assessment of a property to determine if they should purchase it or commit to a specific building project, be it market-rate condominiums or an affordable-housing venture. Zoning lawyers may get involved in the process, but only after the firm has assessed the situation with regards to determining key issues of permissible height, number of units, and building setbacks. Lawyers also directly seek the firm's counsel; Claman, described by partner Davidson as "a larger-than-life graduate of the School of Hard Knocks," recently recalled, "I knew the whole New York City zoning code by heart."

The firm can help a developer complete a deal, and may subsequently serve as the project's architect. Dealing effectively with the city's sometimes-Byzantine building regulations, SLCE has excelled, according to a *New York Times* reporter, at "telling Manhattan apartment developers how to get maximum value out of residential space ... squeezing advantage from necessity." "New York is a tough place to work in," says partner Luigi Russo. "Zoning codes are restrictive and strict. SLCE's expertise in interpreting them has without question been a key factor in its success."

SLCE does not advertise, as most clients approach the firm based on its outstanding reputation. The firm does participate in competitions for affordable housing developments, where it has a solid track record. Unlike many other firms of its size, SLCE had, until very recently, no marketing mechanism. Repeat clients and recommendations from its established client base continue to be the bedrock of the firm's client list.

Among developers, SLCE is well known for its speed, efficiency, and the accuracy of its work. Realistic and well prepared, SLCE navigates a project's schematic design development phase at a pace quicker than industry standard, delivering results in six months, and sometimes even four. The firm's construction documents and administrative work consistently receive positive feedback from the New York City Department of Buildings. As contracts have grown more complex—SLCE began when deals were sealed with a handshake—and a developer's risk of being involved in litigation has increased, the firm's reputation for producing code-compliant initial drawings, and its relationships with municipal agencies amid ongoing changes in both regulations and mayoral administrations, have been invaluable.

Developers often look to SLCE to resolve intricate issues. As partner Robert Laudenschlager has recently observed, "Developers are running out of sites in New York. Today's opportunities are often more difficult and complex than they were 20 years ago. There may be air rights issues or the need to cantilever over existing buildings." Yakas notes that in the 1970s and 1980s buildings were constructed on the basis of a limited number of drawings; now, "green building" requirements and other considerations require separate filings as well as many more meetings, which add significantly to an already costly and time-consuming process. The firm is known for its willingness to get involved with the "nitty-gritty" of the process, adopting a solid client-serving approach.

Over time, developers themselves have become more involved in the design of their own buildings, particularly in the case of large-scale rental projects, such as Queens West, where SLCE has completed close to 4,000 units, many of them rent-regulated, working in conjunction with the Miami-based architectural firm Arquitectonica. The complex public/private project was jointly sponsored by the Port Authority of New York & New Jersey and the New York Empire State Development Corporation, in cooperation with the Queens Borough President. (In 1992, the Queens West Development Corporation was created as an Empire State Development Corporation subsidiary to orchestrate the overall development plan.) Additionally, because the determination of room sizes, floor plans, and finishes all constitute critical decisions

Above: Avalon on the Sound East, New Rochelle, New York

within today's highly competitive market, SLCE works collaboratively with designers to ensure that developers construct buildings that are as responsive to current tastes and requirements as possible.

SLCE is known for its multi-faceted understanding of a project, including its ability to make it cost-efficient, even before cost estimators come on board, as well as for its deep engagement with a building's aesthetics. Claman, who joined SLCE in 1952 as a draftsman and stayed with the firm until he retired in 2009 as a partner, saw buildings and real estate in a practical light: "The most successful job," he stated, "is a handsome building that rents or sells quickly—and is within the cost restraints established by the developer."

RELATIONSHIPS: ARCHITECTURAL COLLABORATIONS

SLCE has long worked in collaboration with high-profile architects such as David Adjaye, Santiago Calatrava, Norman Foster, Zaha Hadid, Bjarke Ingels, Jean Nouvel, César Pelli, Renzo Piano, Robert A.M. Stern, Bernard Tschumi, and Rafael Viñoly. While collaboration can present challenges, SLCE consistently holds firm to its commitment to projects that are both high quality and realizable. SLCE has brought decades of residential experience to joint ventures with these practitioners. Such collaborations, now accounting for 20 percent of the firm's work, have paid significant dividends. As journalist Rich Bockmann has noted, "Robert A.M. Stern and Sir Norman

LAUREATE
2150
LAUREATE
2150

Opposite and left:
The Laureate, New York,
New York

Foster may get all the glory, but SLCE Architects gets all the business." Davidson elaborates, "Where you have a unique property a developer may select an internationally known designer to add a certain cachet from the point of view of sales, or to help a traditional neighborhood get the cachet it deserves. It's a niche we're happy to fill." SLCE partner Luigi Russo, who has collaborated with César Pelli, Helmut Jahn, and Christian de Portzamparc, notes, "These are the people I studied in school."

In the case of collaborations with architects from other countries, or those with little experience of working in New York, SLCE has played an essential role in sharing its deep knowledge of the local market and building processes. As SLCE partner Gloria Glas has stated, "We explain the rules of the game in New York. Here, codes are specific, expectations are specific, and lifestyles are specific."

Two collaborations reflect the breadth of the firm's recent work: the Sugar Hill development and the Woolworth Building. For Sugar Hill, a 13-story, 124-unit building located in an historic enclave within Harlem and completed in 2014, SLCE worked with the London based architect Sir David Adjaye. Designed for low-income individuals and families, the building incorporates extensive amenities, including a 15,000-square-foot children's museum, day-care center, and offices for not-for-profit organizations. Yakas has noted, "The quality of the design and the quality of the finishes has increased tremendously for a lot of low-income housing these days. The expectations of the sponsors and even of city agencies are far greater than they used to be." The budget for Sugar Hill was larger than average, but SLCE and Adjaye still delivered a notably strong impact for the dollar.

Occupying the opposite end of the economic spectrum, SLCE has just finished working with The Office of Thierry Despont on the conversion of the top 30 floors of Cass Gilbert's iconic Woolworth Building (1913) into 33 high-end condominiums. The preservation of the skyscraper's signature neo-gothic terra cotta exterior, which at the time of its completion garnered the building the nickname of the "Cathedral of Commerce," has required technologically complex responses.

SLCE, DESIGN ARCHITECTS

While serving as architect of record on many projects, SLCE's success is also based on its work as principal design architect; the firm has served in that capacity on its affordable housing, school, library, and hospital projects. In the realm of high-end housing, the firm has taken the lead in the design of numerous projects, including Monaco I and II (2017), Halcyon (2014), the Laureate (2011), Avalon on the Sound East (2008), the Avery (2007), and Element (2007). Davidson notes that, "We endeavor to impart each project with its own distinctive personality, its own DNA, in its desire for distinction within its neighborhood."

In 1988 SLCE experienced a watershed moment in its ongoing evolution—from a hardscrabble "developer's firm" to one renowned for its design work—with the completion of the sleek Metropolitan Tower at West 57th Street, strikingly clad in mullion-less dark glass. At that time, New York developers, particularly those focused on residential projects, sought more distinctive "designer" products, each with its own look. For these new projects, which involved complex engineering, the advent of computer-assisted technologies such as CAD improved both design and project management.

SLCE's stellar reputation as design architects has culminated in a number of ground-up design commissions in areas designated as historic districts by the New York City Landmarks Preservation Commission. Davidson has stated that closely working with the commission's staff contributed to the success of projects such as 88 Greenwich and Echelon at 37 West 21st Street.

With the growing sophistication of the Manhattan residential market, developers have sought to add value to their projects. Notes Davidson, "We no longer design apartments. We design lifestyles, incorporating well-curated amenity packages that go beyond the usual gym and yoga spaces to include communal work spaces and media centers." As a result of large high-rise developments being built within high-density Manhattan neighborhoods, buildings often combine at-grade retail, commercial office space, and hotel space. Examples of the firm's mixed-use skyscrapers include Millennium Tower, Thirty Park Place (Four Seasons Hotel), Bloomberg Tower, One57, and 400 Fifth Avenue.

SLCE has also won numerous commissions for stand-alone hotels and commercial office buildings. Hyatt Centric Times Square, Hard Rock Hotel Times Square, 75 Wall Street, Thirty Park Place (Four Seasons Hotel), Moxy, and POD Hotel are all examples of SLCE's increasing portfolio of hospitality commissions. The German Mission to the United Nations, 510 Madison Avenue, and 712 Fifth Avenue are examples of the recent demand for SLCE's office-building expertise.

SLCE has worked extensively with not-for-profit organizations sponsoring affordable housing developments. SLCE's ability to turn out a good product at a good price, backed by a strong commitment to economic diversity and social justice, has led to affordable housing becoming a major part of the firm's work. Widely respected for its knowledge of the financial and legislative underpinnings of such projects, the firm has been able to play an educative role—steering, and in some cases protecting, the sponsoring organizations, which may lack experience with both large-scale architectural projects and the complex world of New York real estate. SLCE is known for its ability to cut through red tape, eliminate unnecessary paperwork, and fully comply with all ordinances. As former partner Al Efron stated, "When the government said, 'We should conduct a study,' I would find a way to end the process right there. I'm a man of action. Just do it."

The Federal Department of Housing and Urban Development (HUD) and the New York City Department of Housing Preservation and Development (HPD) have worked in tandem with SLCE to ensure affordable housing projects proceed smoothly. At the time that the firm began designing public and affordable housing, including projects that fell under the federal government's Section 8 rent-subsidy program and other initiatives, "design" was often a secondary concern. The firm has been able to augment a bare-bones approach, raising standards of amenities and finishes, as well as changing the accepted sizes of units; for instance, the firm succeeded in persuading agencies to increase the maximum allowable size of a one-bedroom unit in an affordable senior residence from 520 square feet to 570 square feet.

A recent example of the firm's low-income housing work is its renovation of the Randolph Houses, a group of Renaissance Revival-style "Old Law" tenements built in the 1890s on West 114th Street in Harlem. The buildings, part of a federally administered National Register of Historic Places, had been acquired by the New York City Housing Authority (NYCHA) during the mid-1970s—when many properties throughout New York were abandoned by their owners and taken possession of by the municipality through an in rem process. In 2016, SLCE won the city's request for proposals with Trinity Financial.

Opposite: Sugar Hill Housing, New York, New York

Pepsi-Cola

Above: SLCE Partners. (From left) Robert Laudenschlager, James Davidson, Gloria Glas, Saky Yakas, Luigi Russo, and Mario Yao, ca. 2012

Opposite: Queens West, Long Island City, New York

Collaborating with NYCHA, with further support provided by federal rehabilitation tax credits, SLCE incrementally gut-renovated the buildings to serve as both public and affordable housing.

Legally mandated preservation restrictions for Randolph Houses presented significant challenges and required difficult compromises. Architecture critic Jonathan Lerner says of SLCE's work that the newly configured units are "spacious and well laid out, with generous interior halls and closets, and abundant natural light." Richard Plunz, architect and author of *A History of Housing in New York City*, adds that, "With all the [project's] downsides, the renovation takes a stand about maintaining Harlem fabric in this moment of huge change, and also maintaining low-income housing ... You've got to admire those architects. They're in the trenches, trying to do something impossible." In 2017, phase I of Randolph Houses earned both the New York Landmarks Conservancy's Lucy G. Moses Award and the Preservation League of New York State's Excellence in Historic Preservation Award.

The Mercy Gardens project in Brooklyn similarly brought together efforts to creatively adapt and reuse neglected buildings with the firm's sensitivity to historic preservation and social commitment. The five-story, 19th-century building, formerly the chief residential facility for the Sisters of Mercy order, was converted into a 78-unit SRO for homeless women. The firm put the project together for Catholic Charities of Brooklyn and Queens. Another related project was for the Mid-Bronx Senior Citizens Council, which converted the Andrew Freedman Home in the Bronx to low-income senior housing. SLCE also successfully converted former hospitals into low-income senior housing in Howard Beach in Queens, and Tuxedo, New York.

SLCE AND THE CITY OF NEW YORK

For more than 75 years, SLCE's role in the development of New York has been multi-dimensional, and both dynamic and enduring. Unflagging in its dedication to quality, SLCE has furthered its artistic goals with efficiency of process and vast expertise in dealing with government agencies and regulations. Above all, SLCE thinks and dreams on a metropolitan scale, ever synthesizing agility, invention, and productivity.

2

MARKET-RATE & LUXURY HOUSING

ONLY

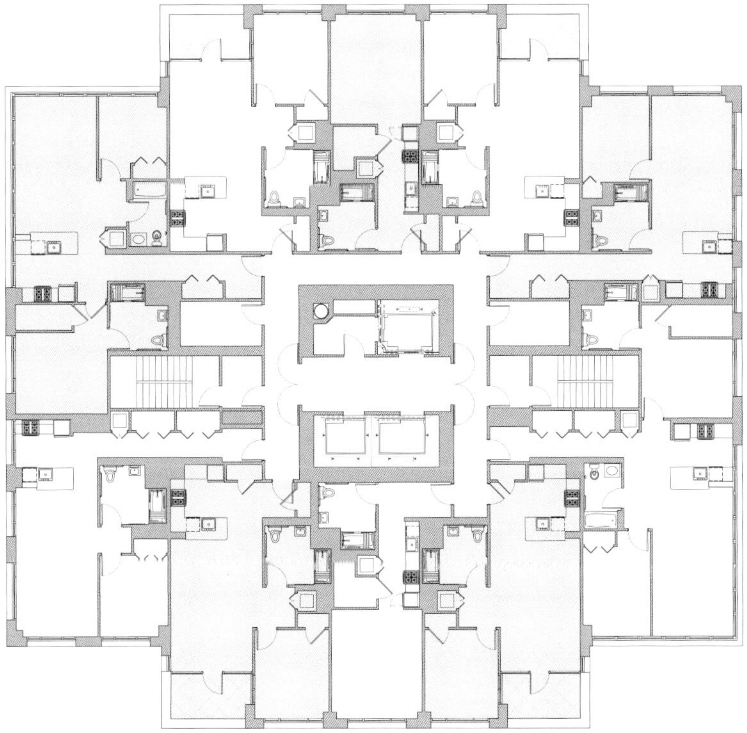

1481 POST STREET

SAN FRANCISCO, CALIFORNIA

RESIDENTIAL TOWER

SLCE Architects has extended its reach nationally with projects throughout the U.S. including the Northeast, Florida, and the West Coast. This 36-story San Francisco project, presently in development, demonstrates SLCE's ability to provide quality projects within aesthetically sensitive urban areas. This site has been envisioned for development for over a decade, and has witnessed numerous schemes fail in planning. SLCE took over the design in 2008 and neared planning approval until the project required redesign for a rental scheme in 2015. Originally planned for 234 luxury condominium units within 36 stories, the redesign comprises 231 rental units within 23 stories. The original amenities were kept and include a roof garden, an indoor swimming pool, and four levels of below-grade parking. Materials for the building's façade were carefully selected to complement San Francisco's predominantly limestone-colored palette.

DEVELOPER:

ADCO Group

EXPECTED COMPLETION:

2021

262 FIFTH AVENUE

NEW YORK, NEW YORK

COLLABORATION, CONDOMINIUM

Rising 1,011 feet tall, 262 Fifth Avenue is a 60-story tower in Midtown Manhattan. The building has two signature exterior elements: the eastern façade will be made from aluminum and glass, with porthole-shaped windows, while the northern and southern façades will have an oversized aluminum and triple-glazed glass curtain-wall system. The building also features a unique vertical core, which will hold all of the mechanics of the building (elevators, egress stairs, etc.). This will allow the apartments to have customizable open floor plans, with expansive, column-free, unobstructed views to the north and south.

The design also fuses the old with the new: the prewar 12-story limestone façade of the neighboring building, 260 Fifth Avenue, forms part of the base of the modern tower of 262 Fifth Avenue.

The top of the tower will feature an arched metal-frame rooftop observation deck for use by residents and their guests.

EXECUTIVE ARCHITECT:
SLCE Architects

DESIGN ARCHITECT:
Meganom

DEVELOPER:
Five Points Development

EXPECTED COMPLETION:
2022

100 EAST 53RD STREET

NEW YORK, NEW YORK

COLLABORATION, MIXED-USE, RESIDENTIAL, RETAIL BASE

In collaboration with Foster + Partners, 100 East 53rd Street is a 63-story, 304,000-square-foot tower with 94 high-end condominium apartments and 9,500 square feet of luxury retail space at the base.

The façade and interior have been designed by Foster + Partners. The exterior is a delicately faceted curtain wall that captures the reflections of the city and complements the Seagram Building, the adjacent modernist landmark. The slender tower is located above a glass podium, responding well to the urban context.

EXECUTIVE ARCHITECT:

SLCE Architects

FAÇADE AND INTERIOR DESIGNER:

Foster + Partners

DEVELOPER:

RFR Holdings, LLC

EXPECTED COMPLETION:

2018

53W53 (MoMA EXPANSION TOWER)

53 WEST 53RD STREET, NEW YORK, NEW YORK

COLLABORATION, MIXED-USE, CONDOMINIUM, MUSEUM EXPANSION

At 82 stories and 505,000 square feet, 53W53 is a 1,050-foot-high tower adjacent to the Museum of Modern Art in Midtown Manhattan. It is programmed to be a mixed-use building that will include a three-story, 50,000-square-foot expansion to the museum's galleries and 120 luxury condominium units with interiors designed by The Office of Thierry Despont.

The building's massing follows closely the zoning envelope of Midtown Manhattan, and its façade expresses the structural bracing required to withstand wind loads. According to the building's design architect, Jean Nouvel, "its sculpted shape was inspired by man's fingers; its innovative 'diagrid' structure soars into the sky." The tower will include an extensive package of amenities including breathtaking New York City and Central Park views, spectacular common areas, and a high-performance fitness facility including a 65-foot lap pool.

DESIGN ARCHITECT:

Ateliers Jean Nouvel

ARCHITECT OF RECORD:

Adamson Associates

RESIDENTIAL ARCHITECT:

SLCE Architects

INTERIOR DESIGNER:

The Office of Thierry Despont

DEVELOPERS:

Hines

Goldman Sachs Real Estate

Pontiac Land Group

EXPECTED COMPLETION:

2019

GREENFORD GREEN

1 BERKELEY AVENUE, GREENFORD, ENGLAND

MIXED-USE, MARKET-RATE RESIDENTIAL, RETAIL

Conceived as a new neighborhood comprising nine new residential buildings and an Art Deco-listed office building flanking a canal running through an abandoned GSK industrial campus, Greenford Green will consist of 1,965 new homes within a mixed-use managed community. SLCE collaborated with HTA Design LLP on a concept masterplan for the site with the focus on creating a vibrant new neighborhood; it will be developed by HTA after planning consent was received in February 2017.

SLCE is responsible for the design and delivery of three buildings on the two blocks south of the canal. The first

block consists of the tallest structure in the scheme at 19 stories, along with a seven-story L-shaped building; these form the gateway to the site, and they comprise 28,320 square feet and 278 market-rate units with retail at the base. The neighboring eight-story, 22,920-square-foot, E-shaped building comprises 233 rental units with amenity spaces of lounges, a gym, dining areas, a cinema, a game room, and work spaces. There are a range of resident terraces and roof gardens overlooking the canal; retail spaces at ground level enliven the canalside.

DEVELOPER:
Greystar Europe Holdings
EXPECTED COMPLETION:
2021

252 EAST 57TH STREET

NEW YORK, NEW YORK

COLLABORATION, MIXED-USE, RENTAL, CONDOMINIUM, RETAIL

252 East 57th Street is located in a block-long site fronting Second Avenue. This 59-story tower, designed by Skidmore, Owings & Merrill (SOM), is a sculpted silhouette characterized by its curved glass façade and balconies that create unique perspectives of the city.

The building contains 169 rental apartments and 93 residential condominiums. Each component has its own lobby and elevators. The 93 residences are enhanced by a thoughtful collection of amenities including a gated porte-cochère, automated parking, 75-foot pool, and 34th Floor Club.

AWARD:

Urban Land Institute Award for Excellence

EXECUTIVE ARCHITECT:

SLCE Architects

DESIGN ARCHITECT FOR THE ENVELOPE:

Skidmore, Owings & Merrill

INTERIORS:

Daniel Romualdez

DEVELOPERS:

WorldWide Group

Rose Associates

COMPLETED:

2016

SAWYER PLACE

LARKIN PLAZA, YONKERS, NEW YORK
MIXED-USE, RESIDENTIAL, RETAIL

Situated in the heart of downtown Yonkers, Sawyer Place offers luxury living a mere 30 minutes from Manhattan. As part of a 586,000-square-foot mixed-use development it features residential units, retail, and parking. The two residential towers, at 25 stories and 17 stories respectively, feature 438 apartments. The commercial and retail components, along with a parking garage, are contained on the lowest three levels across the site. The development offers a variety of amenities, most prominent among them the 18,000-square-foot landscaped roof terrace that offers stunning views of the Hudson River and The Palisades in the distance. Other highlights include attended lobby and concierge services, a resident lounge, fitness center, a private dining and conference room, on-site laundry, and bicycle storage.

The two residential towers were constructed using cast-in-place concrete with an exterior envelope built of light-gauge metal framing with brick veneer and window walls. The two-story retail portion facing the Saw Mill River along Nepperhan Street is of composite deck construction on a steel frame, featuring a full-height curtain-wall storefront. The foundation for the entire site is a pile and mat slab design, which was required due to the high water table and complex soil configuration.

The building is developed in compliance with the Yonkers Green Development guidelines and has many sustainable features throughout, including high-efficiency boilers, energy recovery units for heating and cooling, eco-friendly finishes, and energy-efficient fixtures and appliances. The heating and cooling for the units is achieved with heat pumps off of a central plant located on the building roof.

DEVELOPER:
RXR SoYo Exalta Owner, LLC
EXPECTED COMPLETION:
2019

565 BROOME SOHO

565 BROOME STREET, NEW YORK, NEW YORK

COLLABORATION, MIXED-USE, LUXURY CONDOMINIUM, RETAIL

565 Broome SoHo is a mixed-use, residential condominium of 260,000 square feet and 115 residential units in collaboration with Renzo Piano Building Workshop. The 25-story building envelope consists of a custom-profile aluminum and glass curtain-wall system with curved glass corners to maximize the Hudson River and SoHo neighborhood views.

Among the amenities are an automated parking garage for up to 42 cars, a common swimming pool, fitness center, children's room, sauna, steam room, lounges, and an 80-foot-high conservatory with indoor landscaping and trees. Six duplexes in the setback floor and penthouse levels will have private swimming pools. A private porte-cochère from Broome Street guides the cars to a paved driveway in the inner courtyard. Retail space on the ground and second floors is provided facing Varick, Broome, and Watts Streets.

EXECUTIVE ARCHITECT:
SLCE Architects

DESIGN ARCHITECT:
Renzo Piano Building Workshop

DEVELOPER:
Bizzi & Partners Development

EXPECTED COMPLETION:
2018

220 CENTRAL PARK SOUTH

NEW YORK, NEW YORK

COLLABORATION, CONDOMINIUM

Located in Midtown Manhattan just south of Central Park, 220 Central Park South was designed in collaboration with Robert A.M. Stern Architects. The building consists of two towers comprised of 593,000 square feet and 118 residential units. The main tower stands at 67 stories while the smaller, more residential-scaled tower (known as "The Villas") stands at 18 stories. Both towers are connected by a breezeway which opens onto a plaza-like motor court. The motor court will allow for private resident access within the confines of the property bound by 58th Street and Central Park South. Both towers will share the 30,000 square feet of amenities located at the lower levels—including a 25-meter pool, state-of-the-art fitness center, and spa.

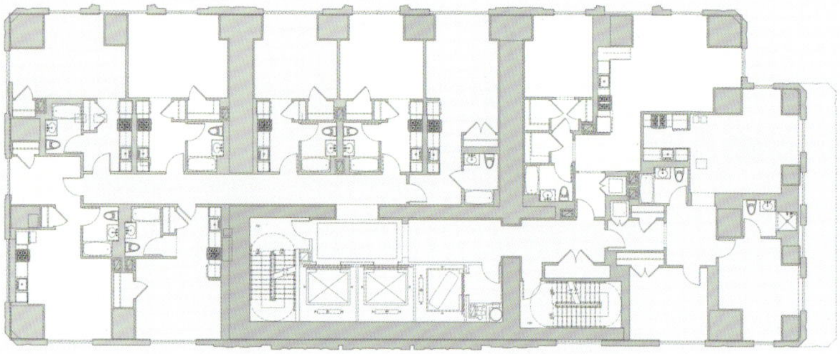

With a tower footprint of 55 feet wide and 130 feet long, the core of the building was shifted to the south in order to provide large living spaces with unobstructed views of Central Park. The introduction of spandrel beams on the perimeter along with ten-inch concrete slabs allowed the structure to work with limited interior columns. The building is clad in three-inch-thick solid limestone panels fabricated on steel trusses and clipped to the superstructure as a standard curtain-wall system. The ability to use this curtain-wall system, in addition to exterior insulation, greatly improved energy efficiency and allowed for more usable floor area. Interior treatments, designed by The Office of Thierry Despont, speak to the traditional language of the exterior façade and massing. Traditional materials, and prominent moldings and details, help define the spaces.

EXECUTIVE ARCHITECT:

SLCE Architects

DESIGN ARCHITECT:

Robert A.M. Stern Architects

INTERIOR DESIGNER:

The Office of Thierry Despont

DEVELOPER:

Vornado Realty Trust

EXPECTED COMPLETION:

2018

520 PARK AVENUE

NEW YORK, NEW YORK

COLLABORATION, CONDOMINIUM

Designed in collaboration with Robert A.M. Stern Architects, 520 Park Avenue is located in the heart of the Upper East Side. The tower's design is in keeping with neighboring buildings, evoking classic New York. In the tradition established by 15 Central Park West, 520 Park Avenue will be entirely clad in Indiana limestone, articulated with hand-set stone detailing reminiscent of the great historic 20th-century apartment houses, but at heights that are truly a modern 21st-century expression. At 54 stories and 200,000 square feet, the building houses 34 luxury units in addition to four amenity floors. The units are comprised of simplex, duplex, and triplex units—all with uninterrupted views of Central Park.

EXECUTIVE ARCHITECT:

SLCE Architects

DESIGN ARCHITECT:

Robert A.M. Stern Architects

DEVELOPERS:

Zeckendorf

Park Sixty

Global Holdings

EXPECTED COMPLETION:

2018

121 E 22ND

121 EAST 22ND STREET, NEW YORK, NEW YORK

COLLABORATION, MIXED-USE, RESIDENTIAL, RETAIL

In collaboration with the Office for Metropolitan Architecture (OMA), SLCE led the team in executing the OMA design while providing interesting residential layouts, without compromising the façade design.

Utilizing the through-block site, SLCE and OMA created two towers connected by a breezeway at the cellar and first floors. The North Tower is 18 stories and consists of 109 luxury residential condominiums, while the South Tower with a smaller footprint contains 25 luxury units and stands 13 stories tall.

Approximately 12,000 square feet of retail space on the ground floor fronts both Lexington Avenue and East 23rd Street; the 213,000 square feet of residential condominiums is situated on the more residential 22nd Street. Residents enjoy an automated parking system that allows them to access their vehicles using a card key or fob. Each of the 24 cars is neatly stacked away on the same "tray" that the resident leaves the car when entering the parking area.

Designed as a standard flat-plate, cast-in-place concrete slab, with transfer slabs on the third and ninth floors, this structure allowed for flexibility of unit layouts while providing a substantial frame for the precast wall system. Introducing a design of one-inch "pleats" in the precast wall, the windows are set deeper at the ends and gradually move out toward the corner, increasing in size. This terminates as a folded façade on the building's corner, and adds desirability to the corner units.

EXECUTIVE ARCHITECT:
SLCE Architects
DESIGN ARCHITECT:
OMA
DEVELOPER:
Toll Brothers City Living
EXPECTED COMPLETION:
2018

THE SUMMIT

222 EAST 44TH STREET, NEW YORK, NEW YORK

COLLABORATION, MIXED-USE, RESIDENTIAL, RETAIL

In collaboration with Handel Architects, The Summit is a 42-story residential rental building in Midtown's Turtle Bay, the latest addition to the densely built streetscape of East 44th Street. The 451,000-square-foot building comprises 429 units, in addition to 2,800 square feet of retail space. In keeping with the trend of combining market-rate and affordable housing in new-construction buildings, 20 percent of the units will rent at below-market rates. Amenities will include concierge and valet services, on-site parking for 230 cars, a penthouse roof deck and lounge, sundeck and barbecue area, indoor swimming pool, resident lounge, golf simulator, children's playroom, fitness center with indoor basketball court, and bike and tenant storage.

EXECUTIVE ARCHITECT:
SLCE Architects

DESIGN ARCHITECT:
Handel Architects

DEVELOPER:
BLDG Management

EXPECTED COMPLETION:
2018

THE MAX

606 WEST 57TH STREET, NEW YORK, NEW YORK

COLLABORATION, MIXED-USE, RESIDENTIAL, RETAIL

Situated at 606 West 57th Street, on the western edge of Hell's Kitchen, The Max will be the third building to be completed in three years on this Hudson River waterfront strip of multi-family rentals that SLCE has worked on as executive and/or design architect.

At 42 stories and 961,000 square feet, the building is comprised of 1,028 units, in addition to 37,000 square feet of commercial space, which will make it one of the largest independent rental developments in New York City. Designed by Arquitectonica, the building is formed of rectangular volumes that stagger inward as it rises, connected through a central vertical core. Amenities available to residents include a roof deck, outdoor theater, clubhouse, fitness center with indoor basketball court, and full-time doorman. The Max will also include parking for 400 vehicles and 558 bicycles.

EXECUTIVE ARCHITECT:
SLCE Architects
DESIGN ARCHITECT:
Arquitectonica
DEVELOPER:
TF Cornerstone
EXPECTED COMPLETION:
2018

POWER HOUSE PERFORMING ARTS THEATER

THE MORGAN AT PROVOST SQUARE

160 MORGAN STREET, JERSEY CITY, NEW JERSEY

MIXED-USE, MARKET-RATE RESIDENTIAL, AFFORDABLE HOUSING, RETAIL, PERFORMING ARTS CENTER

Once complete, The Morgan at Provost Square will consist of four buildings, of which three will be market-rate and one will be affordable housing. At 38, 33, 32 and 28 stories, the 1.6-million-square-foot project will be comprised of 925 units; 32 of these will be affordable and 12 will be designated as live-work units.

Phase 1 was completed in 2014, and comprised 417 units, 16,000 square feet of ground-floor retail, and parking for almost 300 cars. There is residential amenity space on the eighth floor that fronts a landscaped roof terrace with almost 20,000 square feet of roof area, including a green roof, exterior entertaining space, swimming pool, and dog run. The development of subsequent phases 2 and 3 will include a 550-seat performing arts center and 12 live-work units for artists.

The building's façade is designed as a reinforced concrete flat plate with window wall and punched windows in brick and metal panel openings. Since the property is below the base flood elevation, the ground floor has been designed to be dry-flood-proofed with removable storm water gates.

DEVELOPER:

Toll Brothers City Living

PHASE 1 COMPLETED:

2014

FLEET ST
FLATBUSH AVE
GOLD

CITY POINT

10 CITY POINT, BROOKLYN, NEW YORK

COLLABORATION, MIXED-USE, RESIDENTIAL, RETAIL COMPLEX

After a decade of study with the developers of this full city block in downtown Brooklyn in New York City, City Point now stands as a mixed-use multi-building residential and commercial development. At approximately 1,600,000 square feet, City Point is the largest mixed-use development in New York City. SLCE was executive architect on the project, collaborating with COOKFOX Architects to deliver the Commercial Complex and Residential Towers 1 and 2, and then with Kohn Pedersen Fox Associates on Tower 3, known also as 138 Willoughby Street.

The commercial shopping complex, at five stories and 650,000 square feet, is comprised of an interior retail pedestrian street, a large retail vertical core, and an elaborate movie theater with an outdoor terrace.

Residential Tower 1 is 23 stories, 220,000 square feet, and has 314 rental apartment units. Residential Tower 2 stand at 35 stories, boasts 370,000 square feet, and also has 315 rental units. Residential Tower 3 is 53 stories tall, with 250,000 square feet and 458 condominium units.

AWARD:
2017 Excellence in Mixed-Use Development Award, Urban Land Institute in New York State

EXECUTIVE ARCHITECT:
SLCE Architects

COMMERCIAL COMPLEX
DESIGN ARCHITECT:
COOKFOX Architects
DEVELOPERS:
Acadia Realty Trust
Washington Square Partners

RESIDENTIAL TOWER 1
DESIGN ARCHITECT:
COOKFOX Architects
DEVELOPER:
BFC Partners

RESIDENTIAL TOWER 2
DESIGN ARCHITECT:
COOKFOX Architects
DEVELOPER:
Brodsky Organization

RESIDENTIAL TOWER 3
DESIGN ARCHITECT:
Kohn Pedersen Fox Associates
DEVELOPER:
Extell Development Company

COMPLETED:
2017

EAGLE LOFTS

43-22 QUEENS STREET, LONG ISLAND CITY, NEW YORK

COLLABORATION, CONVERSION, RESIDENTIAL

Located in the heart of Long Island City, Eagle Lofts blends the old and new by complementing the newly renovated Eagle Electric Warehouse with a new 54-story residential tower. The entire project offers 790 residential units and over 619,000 square feet of residential and retail area.

The marriage of two very different architectural building typologies has brought about a wealth of unique architectural features that are on display in both the private units and the amenity spaces. The "loft" style apartments in the rehabilitated former warehouse feature exposed concrete columns, 12-foot ceilings, and large windows. The tower apartments offer sweeping views of the Manhattan skyline, courtesy of the largely glass window-wall construction. Amenities include both courtyard and rooftop gardens, a multi-floor fitness center, lounge, children's room, and rooftop pavilion within the original warehouse water tower.

LANDSCAPE DESIGNER:
MNLA

INTERIORS:
SLADE Architecture

DEVELOPER:
Rockrose Development, LLC

EXPECTED COMPLETION:
2018

THE EUGENE

THREE MANHATTAN WEST, 435 WEST 31ST STREET, NEW YORK, NEW YORK

COLLABORATION, MULTI-FAMILY RENTAL WITH INCLUSIONARY HOUSING

The Eugene is the first residential development to rise within the newly created Manhattan West large-scale development located in the Hudson Yards district of Manhattan.

Located on West 31st Street, The Eugene is a 62-story, 730-foot-tall luxury glass tower containing over 800,000 square feet. The façade was designed by renowned architectural firm Skidmore, Owings & Merrill (SOM), with components that include an aluminum and glass curtain wall assembly, custom horizontal metal accent panels, and a bronze horizontal screen wall that defines the residential entrances and sets the tone for the lush residential lobby interiors.

The building contains 844 homes for rent, ranging from 500-square-foot studio units to 1,200-square-foot three-bedroom units, with a portion designated for inclusionary housing. The resident only amenities expected for this level of luxury are provided in over 55,000 square feet of lifestyle and recreational space. These include resident lounges and libraries, a rooftop lounge with stunning Manhattan views, and a full-size gymnasium and fitness center with a 25-foot-tall rock-climbing wall. The sophisticated interiors combine forward-thinking design sensibility with traditional New York appeal, and were detailed by interiors firm RW Studio.

The tower superstructure is poured-in-place concrete with structural steel and concrete on metal deck at the podium levels. Façade components include an aluminum and glass curtain-wall assembly, and metal panel screen walls at selected portions of the podium and bulkhead.

EXECUTIVE ARCHITECT:
SLCE Architects

FAÇADE DESIGN:
Skidmore, Owings & Merrill

INTERIOR DESIGN:
RW Studio

DEVELOPER:
Brookfield Properties

COMPLETED:
2017

THE HAYDEN

43-25 HUNTER STREET, LONG ISLAND CITY, NEW YORK

MARKET-RATE RESIDENTIAL

The Hayden is one of the more recent of many SLCE additions to this actively developing neighborhood, the result of a significant upzoning dating back to before 2001. The Hayden weighs in at 970,000 square feet comprising two towers at 50 and 15 stories, and is home to 974 luxury rental units and 30,000 square feet of amenities including a basketball court, fitness center, laundry room, coffee shop, viewing rooms, lounges, and landscaped terraces with views of the Manhattan skyline.

Every apartment has wooden floors, granite countertops, and stainless steel appliances. Efficient layouts were prepared to maximize the building footprint and to provide a variety of studios and one- and two-bedroom apartments, which often include

generous terraces and balconies. A luxurious two-story lobby connects the mid-rise to the tower via an atrium with a glass skylight that opens to a landscaped court. Ground-floor retail fronting three streets is provided, and the building offers an attended basement parking garage for up to 49 cars.

INTERIOR DESIGNER:
SPaN
DEVELOPER:
Rockrose Development, LLC
COMPLETED:
2017

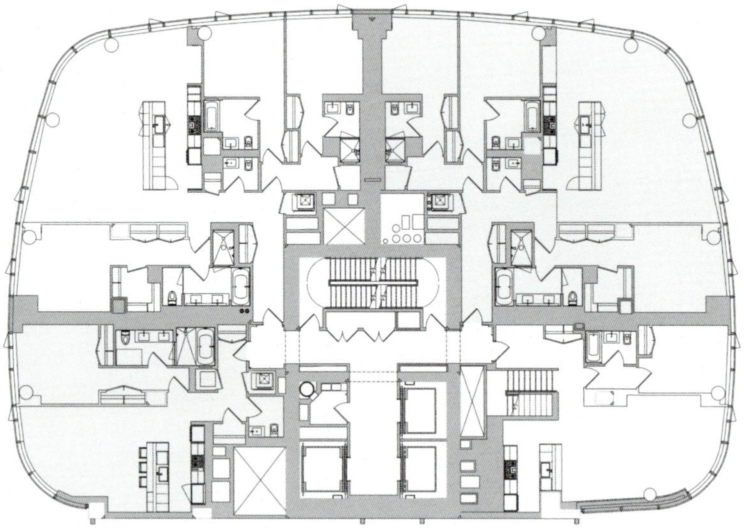

50 WEST STREET

NEW YORK, NEW YORK

COLLABORATION, MIXED-USE, CONDOMINIUM, PUBLIC SPACE

Rising over 780 feet with 527,866 square feet of gross floor area, this 64-story luxury condominium building, designed by Helmut Jahn, features a stainless steel and curved-glass façade, and offers views of New York Harbor, the Statue of Liberty, Ellis Island, the Hudson River, and the East River.

Located in Lower Manhattan's Financial District, 50 West Street consists of 187 residential condominium units. State-of-the-art amenities include a swimming pool, fitness center, children's playroom, private dining room, screening room, library lounge, game room, golf simulator, roof terrace, and an outdoor observation terrace on the 64th floor.

In addition to the amenity spaces, a public plaza of approximately 6,800 square feet is provided adjacent to the building entrance lobby and retail spaces. The public plaza features landscaping, a café, and seating. The plaza serves as the landing of a proposed pedestrian bridge over West Street.

EXECUTIVE ARCHITECT:

SLCE Architects

DESIGN ARCHITECT:

Helmut Jahn

DEVELOPER:

Time Equities Inc.

COMPLETED:

2017

1 QPS TOWER

23–01 42ND ROAD, LONG ISLAND CITY, NEW YORK

RESIDENTIAL

At 44 stories, 1 QPS comprises 391 rental apartment units, ground-floor neighborhood retail, and a large complement of accessory parking. Once a hardscrabble, underutilized industrial area, Long Island City began sprouting dozens of residential high-rise towers starting in 2000, primarily as the result of a major rezoning.

1 QPS is flanked on two sides by an elevated subway, imparting a hip vibe to this new neighborhood, as the building itself resides hard up against a six-story warehouse structure once used primarily to repair taxis and other service vehicles. This 60-foot-tall "blind" space, while unsuitable for residential units, proved ideal for the building's amenity package, which sports 16,000 square feet of fitness center, billiards, a professional rock-climbing wall, library, home-away-from-office space and work areas, communal kitchen, fireplace, and children's playroom; all within a club-like setting. SLCE has contributed at least a dozen buildings and counting since 1996 to this new and vibrant neighborhood lying across the East River from Midtown Manhattan.

DEVELOPER:

Property Markets Group

COMPLETED:

2016

VIA 57 WEST

625 WEST 57TH STREET, NEW YORK, NEW YORK

COLLABORATION, LUXURY RENTAL

Located in the rapidly developing Midtown West neighborhood in Manhattan, VIA 57 West is a stunning and immediately recognizable presence on Manhattan's skyline along the Hudson River. Designed with the Danish architecture firm BIG (Bjarke Ingels Group), the project includes 709 residences—many with terraces and balconies—within 43 stories and 950,000 square feet. SLCE met the challenge to bring this complex project to a successful end, leading the collaborative effort between the client, construction manager, and architectural team.

Conceptualized by BIG as a hybrid between the traditional New York skyscraper and the European perimeter block, the building's design allows for a 22,000-square-foot courtyard garden, and offers sweeping views of the Hudson from a

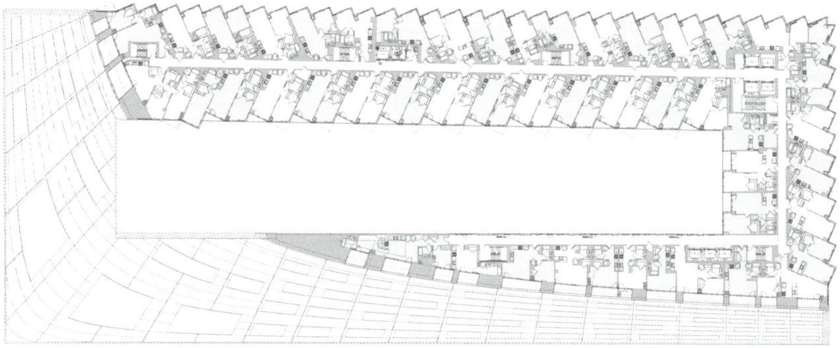

majority of the building residences. Amenities for residents include a swimming pool, fitness center, basketball half-court, golf simulator, children's playroom, library, poker room, media room, and gracious living rooms with fireplace, chef's kitchen, serving kitchen, dining room, and an outdoor terrace with dramatic river views.

The building also features numerous elements geared toward urban sustainability. The energy-efficient building recycles 60,000 gallons of water per day, in addition to using responsibly sourced wood.

AWARDS:

2017 American Institute of Architects (AIA): Housing Award
2016 Society of American Registered Architects (SARA): NY Design Award
2016 Council on Tall Buildings and Urban Habitat: Best Tall Building Award
2016 London Design Museum: Design of the Year
2016 The International Highrise Award
2016 Architect Magazine: Residential Architect Design Award
2015 Architect Magazine: Progressive Architecture Award Citation
2012 AIA New York Chapter: Merit Award for Future Projects

EXECUTIVE ARCHITECT:
SLCE Architects

DESIGN ARCHITECT:
Bjarke Ingels Group

DEVELOPER:
The Durst Organization

COMPLETED:
2016

4FEET 2 INCHES DEEP

AVALON WILLOUGHBY SQUARE

214 DUFFIELD STREET, BROOKLYN, NEW YORK

MARKET-RATE RENTAL

DEVELOPER:

AvalonBay Communities

COMPLETED:

2016

At the time of completion Avalon Willoughby Square was the tallest building in the rapidly expanding neighborhood of Downtown Brooklyn. The building comprises two products unique to the Avalon brand. It is designed to reflect both the refined, sophisticated 'AvalonBay' brand as well as the new, edgy 'AVA' style. The tower, spanning an entire block, has three unique exterior expressions in order to reduce the visual impact and create a more slender expression against an ever-changing skyline. Perhaps the most visually interesting part of the project is the dynamic, pixelated façade that wraps a majority of the building. This element reintroduces a smaller, human-scaled experience that is more typical of the older neighborhood buildings, providing a visually distinctive identity in a market competing for attention. The building totals 57 stories and over 850,000 square feet. The 823 apartments are divided between the AvalonBay and AVA brands, each with its own unique lobby.

THIRTY PARK PLACE FOUR SEASONS HOTEL

30 PARK PLACE, NEW YORK, NEW YORK

COLLABORATION, MIXED-USE, RESIDENTIAL, HOTEL

Designed by Robert A.M. Stern, Thirty Park Place stands an impressive 926 feet high, with 82 stories and sweeping 360-degree views of New York City, including Midtown Manhattan, and the Hudson and East Rivers. With its 157 residences sitting above a Four Seasons Hotel, residential amenities consist of a conservatory and lounge, screening room, children's playroom, fitness center with yoga room, and private dining room.

AWARD:

2017 Excellence in Hotel Development Award, Urban Land Institute in New York State

EXECUTIVE ARCHITECT:

SLCE Architects

DESIGN ARCHITECT:

Robert A.M. Stern Architects

DEVELOPER:

Silverstein Properties Inc.

COMPLETED:

2016

555TEN

555 TENTH AVENUE, NEW YORK, NEW YORK

MARKET-RATE RESIDENTIAL, COMMUNITY FACILITY

555 is a 52-story, 710,000-square-foot tower located in the emerging Hudson Yards area of Manhattan's Midtown West. The building's 598 rental units comprise studio, one-, two-, and three-bedroom apartments, 120 of which are for lower-income households. The building's base houses Success Academy, a K–4 charter school with a dedicated student entrance on West 41st Street.

The building's services and amenities for residents include a 24-hour doorman, concierge, fitness center, tenant storage, rooftop pool, children's playroom, arcade, bowling alley, and pet-care facilities.

DEVELOPER:
Extell Development Company

COMPLETED:
2016

ASTORIA CENTRAL

31-57 31ST STREET, ASTORIA, NEW YORK

RESIDENTIAL RENTAL

Astoria Central is a ground-up, new-construction, seven-story, mixed-use-rate rental project developed by Treeline and Mega Contracting Group. The 114 market-rate residential units in the building are a mix of studios and one-, two-, and three-bedroom apartments on the second to the seventh floors, some with their own outdoor spaces. The building amenities include a doorman, fully equipped fitness center, yoga room, lounge, rooftop terrace with unobstructed views of the Manhattan skyline, second-floor terrace with outdoor kitchen and dining, bicycle parking and storage, and a laundry room. All units have state-of-the-art appliances and kitchens, clean lines, and contemporary finishes.

The ground floor houses 20,000 square feet of retail space with 15-foot clear ceilings and a 3,500-square-foot community facility, spanning between the first and the second floors. The building also includes a 112-car parking garage in the sub-basement.

DEVELOPERS:

Treeline

Mega Contracting Group

COMPLETED:

2016

EŌS

100 WEST 31ST STREET, NEW YORK, NEW YORK

COLLABORATION, MIXED-USE OFFICE, RESIDENTIAL, RETAIL BASE

EŌS is a 47-story mixed-use building offering a residential tower atop a 122,000-square-foot commercial office and 44,000-square-foot retail base. The building features a glass curtain wall designed by COOKFOX Architects, featuring floor-to-ceiling windows and narrow mullions.

The residential tower comprises 375 rental units and occupies floors six to 47, with a 20,000-square-foot outdoor terrace created from the setback of the commercial façade. Twenty percent of the units will be rented at below-market rate, as part of the 421a tax abatement program. The apartments range from studios to three-bedrooms and were designed to compete with market-rate condominiums, featuring high ceilings of nine to ten feet and premium finishes and fixtures. Amenities include a rooftop fireplace, residents' lounge, poker room, and party room.

EXECUTIVE ARCHITECT:

SLCE Architects

DESIGN ARCHITECT:

COOKFOX Architects

DEVELOPERS:

The Durst Organization

Fetner Properties

COMPLETED:

2016

21 WEST END

21 WEST END AVENUE, NEW YORK, NEW YORK

MIXED-USE, RESIDENTIAL, INCLUSIONARY HOUSING, RETAIL, PUBLIC SCHOOL

This mixed-use residential project represents the first of many new buildings comprising the remaining southernmost parcel of the original Riverside South development, a site additionally complicated by an active and functioning below-grade rail line requiring extensive superstructure coordination.

At 43 stories and 768,690 square feet, the building comprises 616 studios and one-, two-, and three-bedroom rental apartments, in addition to 22,000 square feet of retail space, a 117,000-square-foot public school with library and gym (K–8), and a highly curated amenity package that includes a private restaurant, indoor pool, sauna, yoga room, and the usual components of full exercise and wellness programs.

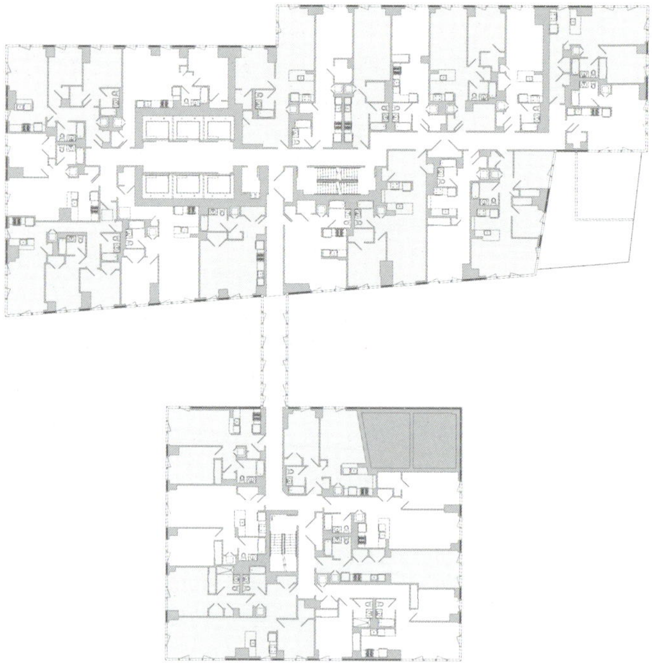

In addition, a full 127 units at 21 West End are dedicated to affordable housing for low-income families. The evolving amenity program of the building has included an archeology exhibition ("The Riverside Project") and is now home to New York City's largest digital sculpture—*Luci.*

INTERIOR DESIGNER:

ICRAVE

DEVELOPER:

Dermot Development Company

COMPLETED:

2016

ONE SIXTY MADISON

160 MADISON AVENUE, NEW YORK, NEW YORK

MIXED-USE, MARKET-RATE AND AFFORDABLE RESIDENTIAL, RETAIL

At 45 stories and 279,387 square feet, One Sixty Madison is a residential tower located in the heart of NoMad at the nexus of Midtown, Gramercy, and Midtown South. The building comprises 319 studios and one- and two-bedroom residences, with specifications and sizes rivaling many neighboring for-sale developments. The building, a poured-in-place concrete structure, features an angled, octagonal design which provides a counterpoint to the typical New York City street grid and is positioned at an angle at the corner of Madison Avenue and 33rd Street, allowing for exciting open views for most residences.

One Sixty Madison features two rooftop amenities—one a passive garden oasis located above the building's retail base, and the other the main roof offering excellent views of Midtown's renowned landmarked office towers.

DEVELOPER:

JD Carlisle Development Corp.

COMPLETED:

2015

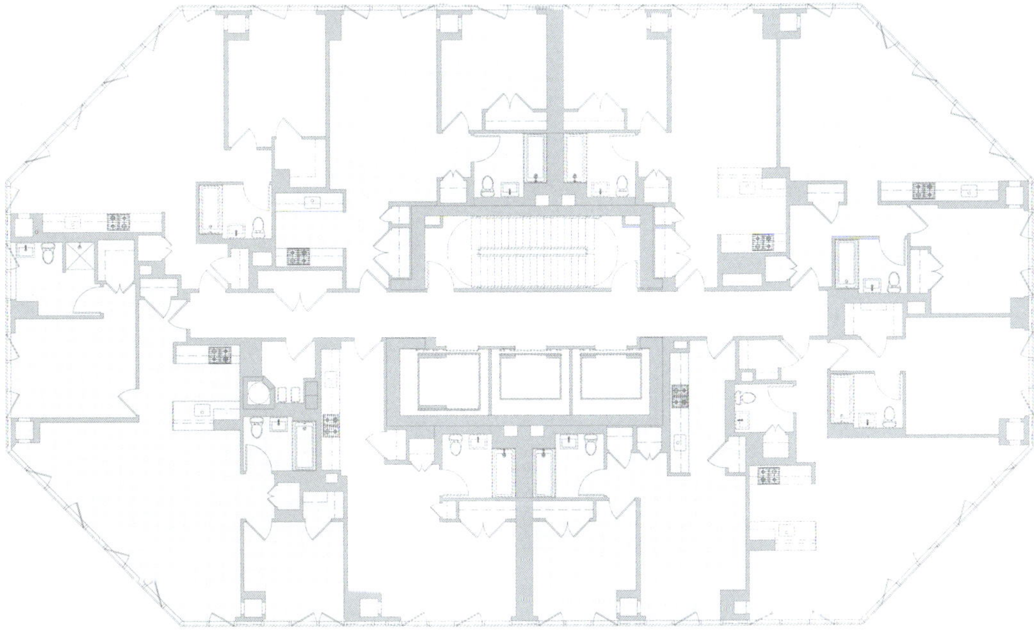

GOTHAM WEST

550 WEST 45TH STREET, NEW YORK, NEW YORK

MIXED-USE, MARKET-RATE RESIDENTIAL, AFFORDABLE HOUSING, CONDOMINIUM & RETAIL BASE, RESIDENTIAL

Gotham West is a complex of four buildings occupying most of the block surrounded by 11th Avenue, 44th Street, and 45th Street. The four independent buildings have different heights: the three build-ups overlooking the streets are 14 stories each and the tower on 11th Avenue—totaling 1.15 million square feet of new construction overlooking a landscaped courtyard—is 31 stories.

The buildings are comprised of 1,404 rental units of both market-rate and affordable housing,

amenity spaces, parking, and a very successful retail space. Previously the site was home to an historic school, which has been renovated as a condominium. A larger school was built in the same block as part of the approval for an extensive rezoning of the site.

DEVELOPER:
Gotham Organization
COMPLETED:
2015

Pepsi-Cola

QUEENS WEST

4-45 47TH ROAD, LONG ISLAND CITY, NEW YORK

MIXED-USE, MARKET-RATE RENTAL, PUBLIC SPACE, RETAIL

In collaboration with Arquitectonica, Queens West consists of seven buildings on a 22-acre waterfront site in Long Island City, on six of which SLCE worked as executive architect. Varying from seven to 35 stories, the masterplan forms an urban edge between the traditional mid-rise structure of Queens and the East River waterfront. The scheme is 3,251,000 square feet and comprises 3,000 residential units and retail, making a strong contribution to this emerging neighborhood.

The six buildings are each designed for different residential markets in apartment types and amenities, including 12 acres of green parks, a children's playroom, tennis courts, sand volleyball courts, landscaped terraces with barbecues, a fitness center, dining rooms, and lounges. Parking is provided in a multi-story garage of 1,000 spaces. Queens West has been selected in several top ten lists for best gyms, best amenities, and best buildings for pets.

EXECUTIVE ARCHITECT:
SLCE Architects
DESIGN ARCHITECT:
Arquitectonica
DEVELOPERS:
TF Cornerstone
Rockrose Development, LLC
COMPLETED:
2014

432 PARK AVENUE

NEW YORK, NEW YORK

COLLABORATION, MIXED-USE, CONDOMINIUM, RENTAL

Located in the center of Manhattan on Park Avenue between 56th and 57th Streets, 432 Park Avenue is the tallest residential building in the western hemisphere. Designed by Rafael Viñoly, this 96-story, 1,396-foot tower provides incomparable residences with spectacular views of Central Park, the Hudson and East Rivers, the Atlantic Ocean, and many iconic Manhattan buildings and avenues. The unencumbered volume of the tower that is located in the center of the block shows a regular grid of exposed concrete members and ten-foot by ten-foot glass windows. The slender tower with its 1:15 ratio is divided into seven equal segments separated by open loggias that expose the building core.

The floor plans, with a floor-to-floor height of 15.5 feet, are free from structural elements and provide for flexibility in the design of the 142 residential units. The lower floors of the building are devoted to amenities for residents, including a private restaurant, a club containing health and spa facilities, a screening room, and a conference center.

The complex also contains a retail and office component with access from 57th Street, the Park Avenue Pavilion, a four-story free-standing commercial building, and a public plaza.

ESSEX
HOUSE

EXECUTIVE ARCHITECT:

SLCE Architects

DESIGN ARCHITECT:

Rafael Viñoly

INTERIORS:

Deborah Berke Partners

DEVELOPERS:

Macklowe Properties

CIM

COMPLETED:

2015

50 UNITED NATIONS PLAZA

NEW YORK, NEW YORK

COLLABORATION, MIXED-USE, LUXURY CONDOMINIUM, RETAIL

This high-rise luxury condominium tower is a joint venture between SLCE and Foster + Partners. The project is located adjacent to the United Nations Plaza across from the United Nations Park, and is next to Dag Hammarskjöld Plaza. The towers' façades incorporate full-height glass curtain walling with large bay windows facing east and west. Views to the east include the East River and the United Nations complex. Views to the west, north, and south include the city skyline and feature the Chrysler Building to the southwest, among other iconic NYC landmarks. The project includes a large health club and spa featuring a full-size lap pool and modern amenities including parking, a wine cellar, and retail at the base.

EXECUTIVE ARCHITECT:

SLCE Architects

DESIGN ARCHITECT:

Foster + Partners

DEVELOPER:

Zeckendorf Development

COMPLETED:

2015

OCEANA

135 OCEANA DRIVE EAST, BRIGHTON BEACH, BROOKLYN, NEW YORK

COLLABORATION, CONDOMINIUM

Oceana is an 865-unit residential development built as a network of "neighborhood-scaled" streets on a 15-acre site in the Brighton Beach neighborhood of Brooklyn, New York. The community initially had 15 buildings, designed in collaboration with SB Architects beginning in 1999, with a 16th building completed in 2014. This strategy allowed for any adjustments dictated by market demand.

Oceana has an array of recreational facilities, including a swim club, private beach access, landscaped grounds, a fully equipped and staffed health club, and a 6,500-square-foot event space and spa. Units feature high ceilings, panoramic city views, washer/dryer units, marble baths, and chefs' kitchens, and residents benefit from 24/7 security and 1,200 underground parking spaces.

AWARDS:

2001 Long Island Builders Institute Award

2002 Brooklyn Chamber of Commerce Building Brooklyn Award

2003 National Association of Home Builders Multi-Family Best For-Sale Housing Award

2004 National Sales and Marketing Council Best Homes Award

2007 Brooklyn Chamber of Commerce Building Brooklyn Award

EXECUTIVE ARCHITECT:

SLCE Architects

DESIGN ARCHITECT:

SB Architects

DEVELOPER:

Muss Development

COMPLETED:

2008–2014

250N10

250 NORTH 10TH STREET, BROOKLYN, NEW YORK

MARKET-RATE RESIDENTIAL

250N10 is a six-story, 237,285-square-foot building with a curved façade designed by SLCE in the Williamsburg district of Brooklyn. Its cutting-edge exterior design addresses a younger demographic, often entering the job market for the first time. The building has 233 rental units, which are a mix of one- and two-bedroom apartments, usually addressing the shared market. Amenities stress interaction and community for those who might have only recently graduated and who are attracted to this vibrant, edgy neighborhood.

The main street façade turns a gentle corner and is articulated with stepped color-banded horizontal elements. The semi-recessed 116-space parking facility raises the ground level to provide defensible space and allows double-height amenity spaces. In addition, the building boasts over 10,000

Union
TRUCK ROUTE
LOCAL

square feet of amenity space, comprised of a 24-hour lounge, outdoor courtyard, entertainment lounge on the top floor, and rooftop terrace.

As the Manhattan market has matured and become increasingly inaccessible to young and talented professionals, both in the burgeoning technology sector and in the arts, SLCE has increasingly been tasked with the design of major residential buildings in new neighborhoods in Brooklyn and Queens, which afford easy subway access to the city across the East River. This market has demonstrated consistent growth over the last few decades, which is only expected to continue with New York's ongoing resurgence.

DEVELOPER:
LCOR
COMPLETED:
2014

AVALON WEST CHELSEA

282 11TH AVENUE, NEW YORK, NEW YORK

COLLABORATION, MIXED-USE, RENTAL, RETAIL

In collaboration with Fogarty Finger, Avalon West Chelsea is an L-shaped red-brick residential building located at 282 11th Avenue, and is part of the AVA High Line complex. At 27 stories and 675,000 square feet, this rental building comprises 691 market-rate units, offering studios and one- and two-bedroom apartments. The retail base of the building contains a 21,000-square-foot Union Fare "gastrohall" of food and beverage vendors, a lounge, and a gallery.

Other amenities include a state-of-the-art fitness center, terrace, and residents' lounge.

EXECUTIVE ARCHITECT:

SLCE Architects

DESIGN ARCHITECT:

Fogarty Finger

DEVELOPER:

AvalonBay Communities

COMPLETED:

2014

MAXWELL PLACE

BUILDING "C," 1025 MAXWELL LANE, HOBOKEN, NEW JERSEY

MIXED-USE, RESIDENTIAL, RETAIL

The third building of a planned four-building development, Building "C" of Maxwell Place on the Hudson River is 12 stories and 309,000 square feet, including 25,000 square feet of ground-floor retail space. It is comprised of 210 residential units and 374 parking spaces and provides parking for the future fourth structure. Roof terraces for the residential units can be found on the seventh floor setback and above the 12th floor.

With a maximum building height of 125 feet, and as a reflection on the past, this building fits into the fabric of Hoboken's older neighborhoods. The site was once the home of Maxwell House coffee, and is one city block long. Its 400-foot-long façade is articulated to break down the length to human scale, and this helps define the retail spaces at street level.

Using brick and a combination of punched and window wall, with a structural stud backup wall, the insulation in the cavity helps increase energy efficiency.

DEVELOPER:
Toll Brothers City Living

COMPLETED:
2014

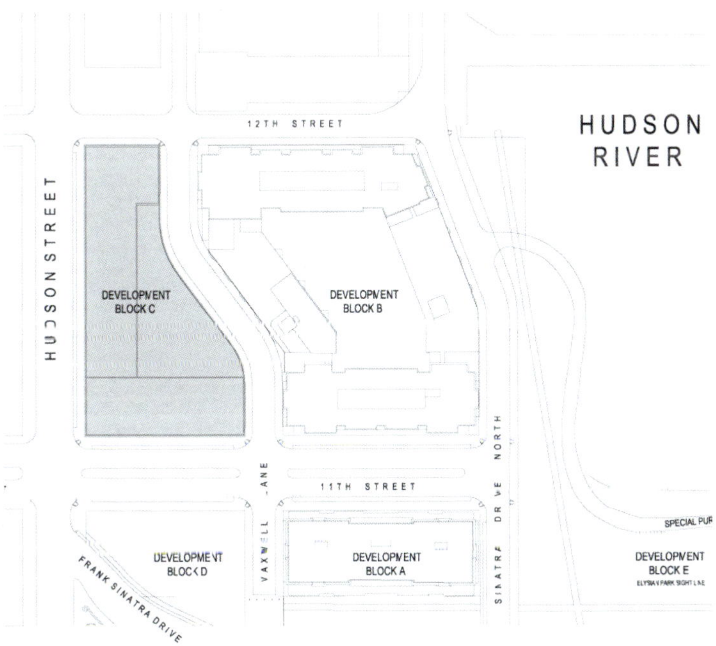

THE PEARSON COURT SQUARE

45-56 PEARSON STREET, LONG ISLAND CITY, NEW YORK

MARKET-RATE HOUSING

The Pearson Court Square, located in Long Island City, Queens, is a new-construction, 15-story, 170,000-square-foot building comprised of 197 market-rate rental apartments. Tenant amenities include a fitness center, yoga studio, and exterior common terraces at the roof, tenth, and second floors. The side yard features a landscaped space with a bocce court and a basketball half-court.

The building was constructed with concrete block and precast concrete planks, sitting atop a one-story poured-in-place concrete plinth. The building exterior speaks to the surrounding neighborhood's warehouse style through a combination of architectural face brick and insulated aluminum composite metal panels alongside historical-style windows. The building also features a grand double-height lobby, and all amenity spaces have direct access to outdoor terraces. The apartment interiors feature full-height windows for expansive views across the East River to Manhattan, along with modern finishes in both kitchens and baths.

Sustainability was integral to the building's design, leading it to receive LEED Silver certification. The building's roof features a series of three vertical-axis wind turbines that power the roof lounge and aid in offsetting the building's energy footprint.

DEVELOPER:
L&M Development Partners

COMPLETED:
2014

SEMZ IZ THE WIZ

2 Av

HALCYON

303 EAST 51ST STREET, NEW YORK, NEW YORK

MIXED-USE, RESIDENTIAL, RETAIL

At 32 stories and 265,000 square feet, Halcyon comprises 123 luxury condominium apartments, ground-floor retail space, accessory parking, and an unusual indoor pool and amenity package positioned in the middle of the tower, a result of nuances in zoning resolution text.

Halcyon was the third of a number of towers designed by SLCE in this particular Midtown location; it presents a warmer palette of limestone and bronze tones on a limestone-clad base, relating in scale to the neighborhood's tree-lined side-street walk-ups. The tower portion that fronts Second Avenue presents a more glass-and-metal materiality shared by the many new buildings which have sprung up within the same timeframe.

Amenities include a mid-tower 52-foot indoor two-lane pool featuring a spa and sauna, health club, library, residents' lounge with catering kitchen, yoga studio with double-height windows, and a double-height entrance lobby.

DEVELOPER:

HFZ Capital Group

COMPLETED:

2013

388 BRIDGE STREET

BROOKLYN, NEW YORK
RENTAL, CONDOMINIUM

Located in downtown Brooklyn, 388 Bridge Street is among a cohort of new residential towers in the neighborhood. The building held the record for tallest building in Brooklyn until the development of Avalon Willoughby Square, also designed by SLCE. At 53 stories and 413,000 square feet, the building is comprised of 357 units, all with nine-foot ceilings. Additionally, the ground floor features 10,500 square feet of retail space and an athletic club. The fifth floor features a dedicated amenity space along with an outdoor recreation space for residents.

The building was designed with a reinforced concrete flat-plate system and introduced "belt" walls at the mechanical levels, which help provide lateral reinforcing. Utilizing a window-wall system of aluminum, glass, and metal panels, the façade was simplified to be visually seamless. The façade is comprised of different glass types, which reflect the light at varying planes.

DEVELOPER:
Stahl Real Estate
COMPLETED:
2013

W 76 St

THE LAUREATE

2150 BROADWAY, NEW YORK, NEW YORK

MIXED-USE, CONDOMINIUM, RETAIL

This 18-story, 300,000-square-foot luxury condominium building comprising 75 apartments, neighborhood retail, and a car rental agency is located in the heart of Manhattan's Upper West Side. The Laureate's design is a response to the scarcity of Beaux-Arts edifices, which once populated this part of town but increasingly gave way to the many nondescript postwar exercises of the 1960s and 1970s. After the developer shared a vision of revisiting this aesthetic, SLCE seized on the opportunity to design a limestone exterior rich in detail, decorative railings, Juliet balconies, and 10-foot-high ceilings.

Inside the Laureate speaks to the upper end of the Manhattan residential market with grandly proportioned great rooms, oversized kitchens and pantries, and high-end specifications throughout. Comprising one- to six-bedroom units, and amenity spaces which include a music room, children's playroom, private dining room, and exercise room opening onto a private landscaped yard, the Laureate fills an essential niche in this family-oriented neighborhood.

DEVELOPER:
The Stahl Organization

COMPLETED:
2013

ONE57

153 WEST 57TH STREET,
NEW YORK, NEW YORK

*COLLABORATION, MIXED-USE,
CONDOMINIUM, HOTEL*

In collaboration with Christian de Portzamparc Architects, at 72 stories and 850,000 square feet, One57 comprises 135 residential condominium units and a 210-room Park Hyatt. Apart from Metropolitan Tower, which was designed by SLCE and completed in 1986, the 57th Street corridor of Manhattan remained dormant in significant residential development for over 20 years.

By 2010, the development climate was ripe for new, tall structures, with price tags for residential units clearing the $10,000 per square foot threshold. One57 was the first to market in

2013 along this broad thoroughfare, now branded "Billionaires' Row," and was the first of many to redefine the skyline as viewed from Central Park. SLCE provided its extensive residential planning and technical expertise to this complex project in the role of executive architect.

EXECUTIVE ARCHITECT:
SLCE Architects
DESIGN ARCHITECT:
Christian de Portzamparc Architects
DEVELOPER:
Extell Development Company
COMPLETED:
2013

MAXWELL'S
BAR
& RESTAURANT

57 READE STREET

NEW YORK, NEW YORK

MIXED-USE, RESIDENTIAL, RETAIL BASE

57 Reade Street is located in a transitional part of Lower Manhattan, on the edge of the Tribeca historic district, across from the Department of Buildings and generally surrounded by office structures dating from the 1950s and later. The building's complex massing is the result of its interface with two divergent zoning districts, yet it still manages to reach a height of 20 stories fronting Broadway. Weighing in at 142,000 square feet, 57 Reade Street comprises 84 condominium apartments, two levels of above-grade retail space, two retail basements, and a complement of amenities appropriate for its relatively small size. In keeping with the pioneering aspect of a for-sale development in this edgy part of Manhattan, the building's exterior reflects its neighborhood, providing abundant light and views for its inhabitants with a primarily glass window wall.

DEVELOPER:

The John Buck Company

COMPLETED:

2012

135
135

135 EAST 79TH STREET

NEW YORK, NEW YORK

COLLABORATION, CONDOMINIUM

135 East 79th Street is a 19-story luxury condominium located in the heart of Manhattan's Upper East Side. Designed as a classic New York City building, it possesses the elegance of modern luxury living, with a hand-laid brick and limestone exterior, and a limestone ornamental and relief sculpture entrance. The building also has a custom-designed wood crown molding, base, and interior door trims.

This luxury building consists of a total of 32 apartments that include two maisonettes with private gardens and six duplex penthouses with private terraces. The upper floor units have a private entry foyer and access to a service corridor and elevator. Amenities include a fitness center with a private training studio, residents' lounge, children's playroom, and an outdoor garden.

EXECUTIVE ARCHITECT:
SLCE Architects
DESIGNER:
Studio Sofield
DEVELOPER:
The Brodsky Organization
COMPLETED:
2012

1500, 1501 & 1510 LEXINGTON AVENUE

NEW YORK, NEW YORK

MIXED-USE, RESIDENTIAL, RETAIL

SLCE worked closely with the developer, community groups, the Department of City Planning, and land-use attorneys to successfully upzone this now-vibrant neighborhood flanking Lexington Avenue from underperforming density. Starting with 1501, then moving across the avenue to 1500 and up the block to 1510 Lexington Avenue, each of the buildings' complex massings responds to the different zoning densities residing on each development lot. Each of the buildings was designed with a focus on market-rate rentals, the demand for which had moved north of 96th Street at this time and included health clubs,

BARBER SHOP

party and game rooms, and neighborhood-oriented retail spaces. While the first building was circumspect in its ambitions, the later buildings were more sophisticated both in design and amenities on offer as the neighborhood matured. SLCE provided full architectural design, technical, and interior design services for these projects.

DEVELOPER:
Kenbar Management
COMPLETED:
2011

MONACO I & II

475 WASHINGTON BOULEVARD, JERSEY CITY, NEW JERSEY

CONDOMINIUM

Located on the full block fronting Washington Street between Thomas Gangemi Drive and Fourth Street, this development received planning consent for three towers encircling an existing Double Tree hotel in 2008, the first two of which were christened Monaco I and II and completed in 2011, with San Remo, a planned third tower, due to commence development in 2018. Monaco I and II comprise two slender 50-story towers clad in limestone and matching brick, accentuated with floor-to-ceiling glass corners and feature prow.

Atop the parking structure resides a full complement of amenities, including a rooftop sundeck with heated open-air pool, fitness center, spa, fireside lounge, theater, and club room with billiards. Most of the apartments enjoy panoramic views of the Manhattan skyline across the road toward the Hudson River and New York Harbor.

Monaco I and II were SLCE's fifth and sixth of ten (and counting) towers along this stretch of Jersey City, with convenient access to the light rail and PATH stations.

LANDSCAPE DESIGNER:
Melillo and Bauer Associates

DEVELOPER:
Roseland Residential Trust

COMPLETED:
2011

ONE JACKSON SQUARE

122 GREENWICH AVENUE, NEW YORK, NEW YORK

COLLABORATION, MIXED-USE, LUXURY CONDOMINIUM, RETAIL

Located in the Greenwich Village historic district in Lower Manhattan, One Jackson Square is an 11-story, 60,000-square-foot building which features 35 luxury condominiums.

Designed in collaboration with Kohn Pedersen Fox, the building complements its surrounding structures; its curved glass façade as well as unusual apartment layouts are a response to the wedge shape of the site and to the various zoning requirements of the property. The building also includes retail space as well as residential amenity spaces, totaling 7,300 square feet on the ground floor and basement levels.

AWARDS:

Sustainable Design Award for the development of New York's first LEED-certified luxury condominium

Commendation in the MIPIM Architectural Review: Future Project Award in the residential category

Silver Award for Engineering Excellence

2011 Honor Award for Architecture, American Institute of Architects (AIA)

2013 Honor Award, American Institute of Architects (AIA)

2010 Award of Merit: Residential Large Projects, AIA New York

2010 Urban Contextual Award, Society of American Registered Architects NY

2010 American Architecture Award, The Chicago Athenaeum

2010 Merit Award for Multi-Family Residential, New York City Construction Awards

EXECUTIVE ARCHITECT:

SLCE Architects

DESIGN ARCHITECT:

Kohn Pedersen Fox Associates

DEVELOPER:

Hines

COMPLETED:

2011

AZURE

333 EAST 91ST STREET, NEW YORK, NEW YORK

MIXED-USE, MARKET-RATE CONDOMINIUM, PUBLIC SCHOOL

Located in the Yorkville neighborhood of the Upper East Side and a stone's throw from the East River and Carl Schurz Park, Azure's 34 stories stand among an increasing number of similarly scaled towers along First Avenue.

Built as a condop (a coop with condominium rules, built on leased property) many of its original 128 apartment units were combined by the developer after initial rollout to fufill the increasing need for larger, four-bedroom apartments in this maturing neighborhood, with no more than four units per floor.

The building's limestone-colored, split-faced brick piers and floor-to-ceiling window wall complement this recently revitalized neighborhood. The building's 7,000 square feet of amenities include a rooftop club and landscaped outdoor deck, game room, lounge and event space, fitness center, and private dining facility with adjoining catering kitchen.

An important component of this development, which enabled the project to move forward, was the integration of a public-school structure located at the building's base.

DEVELOPER:

The De Matteis Organization

COMPLETED:

2010

ONE MUSEUM MILE

1280 FIFTH AVENUE, NEW YORK, NEW YORK

COLLABORATION, MIXED-USE, MUSEUM, LUXURY CONDOMINIUM

Located at the northeast corner of Central Park and Duke Ellington Circle, this mixed-use condominium project provides the terminus of the long march of stately Fifth Avenue properties. The 19-story building, known as 1280 Fifth Avenue, has 116 residential condominiums. The northern, low-rise portion of the building contains the Museum of African Art, which was founded in 1984 by Susan Mullen Vogel.

EXECUTIVE ARCHITECT:
SLCE Architects

DESIGN ARCHITECT:
Robert A.M. Stern Architects

DEVELOPER:
Brickman

COMPLETED:
2010

THE VISIONAIRE

70 LITTLE WEST STREET, NEW YORK, NEW YORK

COLLABORATION, LUXURY CONDOMINIUM

The Visionaire has been designed in compliance with the Battery Park City Authority Residential Environmental Guidelines and has received U.S. Green Building Council LEED Platinum certification with optimum energy efficiency and indoor air quality, and waste water management.

AWARD:

2009 American Institute of Architects, New York Chapter/Boston Society of Architects Building Type Honor Award for Housing

EXECUTIVE ARCHITECT:

SLCE Architects

DESIGN ARCHITECT:

Pelli Clarke Pelli Architects

DEVELOPER:

The Albanese Organization

COMPLETED:

2006

CHELSEA STRATUS

101 WEST 24TH STREET, NEW YORK, NEW YORK

CONDOMINIUM

At 38 stories and 323,000 square feet, Chelsea Stratus is the first for-sale tower within this neighborhood to be built along this Sixth Avenue corridor between 23rd and 34th Streets, comprising 204 apartment units. With its balconies, cast-stone façades, and undulating glass window wall, this luxury condominium stands elegantly against its brick-clad market-rate rental neighbors. The building's many amenities include an indoor basketball court, health club, and a beautifully landscaped second-floor roof deck.

Utilizing development rights and a light and air easement, the building was constructed with a 25-foot cantilever over the neighboring property to the west. This activated the ability to use 37,000 square feet of zoning area. Comprised of precast elements and a window-wall system consisting of inswing casement windows, the developer was able to eliminate the need for a façade maintenance unit.

DEVELOPER:

LCOR Incorporated

COMPLETED:

2008

111 CENTRAL PARK NORTH

NEW YORK, NEW YORK

COLLABORATION, CONDOMINIUM

Located in Harlem on the north edge of Central Park, 111 Central Park North is a new-construction residential building. Designed in collaboration with Hillier Architecture, the building is intended to offer uncompromised park views in the spirit of the neighborhood's laidback character. To this end, each condominium features a balcony facing the park, contributing to the notion of seamless indoor-outdoor living. Floor-to-ceiling windows allow for an abundance of natural light and a transparent façade. At 19 stories and 140,000 square feet, the building is comprised of 48 units. Amenity spaces include a 10,000-square-foot terrace in addition to 9,000 square feet of retail space.

EXECUTIVE ARCHITECT:

SLCE Architects

DESIGN ARCHITECT:

Hillier Architecture

DEVELOPER:

The Athena Group

COMPLETED:

2008

HUDSON PARK

1 ALEXANDER STREET,
YONKERS, NEW YORK
MARKET-RATE HOUSING

DEVELOPER:
Collins Enterprises, Inc.
COMPLETED:
2008

Hudson Park is a waterfront development in Yonkers, New York on the banks of the Hudson River and adjacent to the Yonkers Metro-North station.

Phase I, a U-shaped, nine-story, 311,400-square-foot building, contains 272 apartments, parking for 300 cars, and retail space on the ground floor. Phase I was completed in October 2003.

Phase II, Hudson Park North, consists of a 14-story, 330,400-square-foot building which houses 294 apartments and a separate five-story parking structure for 430 cars. A landscaped riverfront promenade connecting the buildings completed the project. The second phase of Hudson Park was completed in March 2008.

THE DYLAN

309 FIFTH AVENUE, NEW YORK, NEW YORK

MIXED-USE, MARKET-RATE RENTAL, RETAIL

Built in the heart of Midtown, The Dylan is a 34-story rental building which has 165 luxury apartments ranging from studios to two-bedrooms. The building is 175,000 square feet, including 10,000 square feet of retail space at the building's base. Amenities include a fitness center, indoor basketball court, bike storage, and a rooftop lounge and terrace.

DEVELOPER:

Urban Development Partners

COMPLETED:

2008

170 EAST END AVENUE

NEW YORK, NEW YORK
COLLABORATION, CONDOMINIUM

With spectacular views of the East River, 170 East End Avenue is a 19-story dynamic high-end luxury condominium on New York's Upper East Side. The building contains 198 apartments, some of which have fireplaces and balconies. Among the many amenities are an extensive family center, parking garage, and a landscaped courtyard featuring a sculpted water wall.

EXECUTIVE ARCHITECT:
SLCE Architects
DESIGN ARCHITECT:
Peter Marino
DEVELOPER:
Skyline Developers
COMPLETED:
2009

THE CHRYSTIE & AVALON BOWERY PLACE I & II

229 CHRYSTIE STREET AND 11 EAST FIRST STREET, NEW YORK, NEW YORK

COLLABORATION, MIXED-USE, RENTAL, COMMUNITY FACILITY, RETAIL

SLCE Architects was executive and residential architect for The Chrystie (formely Chrystie Place) and Avalon Bowery Place I and II on a multi-city-block site, designed in phases over five years and fully completed in 2014. The entire development parcel was awarded to AvalonBay Communities by NYC Housing Preservation and Development as a major revitalization to this portion of the Lower East Side.

Avalon Bowery Place considerably augmented this neighborhood's density, strategically located at the intersection of Houston and Bowery, just south of Manhattan's East Village. The three buildings were designed and constructed in three phases. Phase I is a 14-story, 395,000-square-foot mixed-use building with 361 residential units, ground- and second-floor retail, and a YMCA. The residential building has a landscaped deck, fitness center, and residents' lounge. Phase II (Bowery Place I, pictured) is a nine-story, 238,000-square-foot mixed-use building with 206 units, ground-floor retail, a garage, residential landscaped deck, a fitness center, and lounge. Phase III (Bowery Place II) is a seven-story, 115,000-square-foot mixed-use building with 96 units, ground-floor retail, a garage, residential landscaped deck, and residential lounge. The entire assemblage allowed for more robust retail and ultimately included a Whole Foods and other much-needed neighborhood and community services.

AWARD:

2009 Big Apple Brownfield Award, The New York City Brownfield Partnership

EXECUTIVE & RESIDENTIAL ARCHITECT:

SLCE Architects

DESIGN ARCHITECT:

Arquitectonica

DEVELOPER:

AvalonBay Communities

COMPLETED:

The Chrystie and Bowery Place I – 2008

Bowery Place II – 2014

BOWERY PLACE
LEASING OFFICE
LEASING OFFICE
Retail Space Available
www.AvalonBoweryPlace.com

AVALON ON THE SOUND EAST

255 HUGUENOT STREET,
NEW ROCHELLE, NEW YORK
MARKET-RATE RENTAL

At 40 stories and 834,000 square feet, the building is comprised of 588 rental units. Working with the City of New Rochelle, the project continues an effort to redefine this historic city, and includes a stand-alone five-story parking structure to aid in the city's development. The tower includes a rooftop lounge with sweeping views of the New York City skyline and Long Island Sound.

The mass of the building is broken down into simple blocks, with glass façade elements increasing along the corners of each wing of the two-wing tower, as the tower grows vertically. A mid-height setback helps to enhance the building's presence on the skyline.

The superstructure is poured-in-place concrete, and façade components include an aluminum and glass window-wall assembly, hand-laid brick cavity wall, and natural stone accents at the street level.

DEVELOPER:
AvalonBay Communities
COMPLETED:
2008

4 FEET 2 INCHES DEEP
NO DIVING

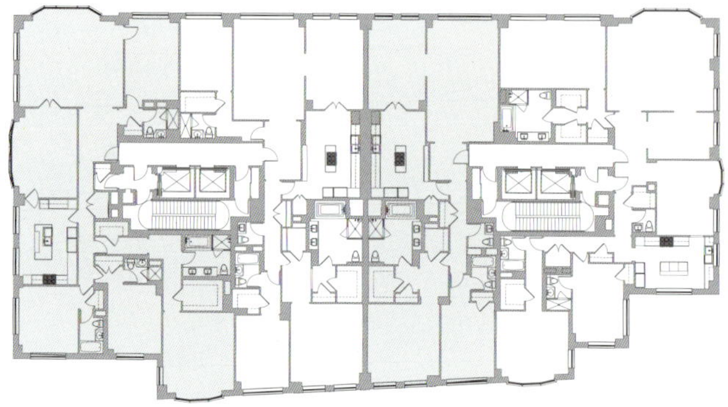

15 CENTRAL PARK WEST

NEW YORK, NEW YORK

COLLABORATION, CONDOMINIUM

Fronting both Central Park West and Broadway, the result of a truncated trapezoidal block, 15 Central Park West's site lay vacant for over a decade, with a tired but storied Mayflower Hotel falling further into disrepair over the years. Although SLCE worked for years with many developers trying to make a deal with the landowner, it was Zeckendorf Development which finally came up with the winning bid, owing to SLCE's development of a full set of plans and general massing concepts that instilled a high level of confidence, allowing the deal to move forward. Subsequently, the developer engaged Pelli's and Robert A.M. Stern's offices to develop alternative design concepts for the façade. Stern's office won the day with a limestone façade with flourishes of detail evoking a prewar aesthetic; a convincing and successful formula used many times since within that firm's repertoire.

The development comprises two buildings flanking a formal motor court and garden; the "house" which fronts Central Park, and a major 35-story tower which addresses Broadway to the west. One massing concept which was developed by the owner and SLCE early in the planning phase was the raising of the tower above the "house" to maximize views toward Central Park, a feature allowed by the zoning text for towers not bound by height constraints within this zoning district. The 231 luxury residences—which were the first to cross the $3,000 per square foot bar—range from oversized one-bedroom apartments to full-floor and terraced duplex penthouses. The building also features 85,000 square feet of retail space at the ground level fronting Broadway, and unparalleled amenities including a below-grade sky-lit pool and below-grade parking.

EXECUTIVE ARCHITECT:
SLCE Architects

DESIGN ARCHITECT:
Robert A.M. Stern Architects

DEVELOPER:
Zeckendorf Development

COMPLETED:
2008

THE EPIC

125 WEST 31ST STREET, NEW YORK, NEW YORK

COLLABORATION, MIXED-USE, MARKET-RATE RENTAL, OFFICE BUILDING, HEALTHCARE

The Epic is a 58-story mixed-use building in Manhattan's Midtown West neighborhood. The tower contains 470 apartments, ranging from studios to two-bedroom apartments spanning the building's 580,000 square feet. In addition to a full range of affordable and market-rate residential units, The Epic's complex program includes the New York offices of the American Cancer Society as well as the Hope Lodge Hospice, a separate wing of St. Francis of Assisi Church and Friary. The Epic is one of an increasing number of SLCE projects receiving LEED certification.

EXECUTIVE ARCHITECT:
SLCE Architects

DESIGN ARCHITECT:
FxFowle

DEVELOPER:
Fetner Properties

COMPLETED:
2008

LEED Gold Certified Building

305W16

305 WEST 16TH STREET, NEW YORK, NEW YORK

RESIDENTIAL CONDOMINIUM

Located in West Chelsea close to the Meatpacking District and the High Line—which revitalized this neighborhood into a destination for art and sculpture galleries and eateries—305 West 16th Street joins a growing number of edgy, groundbreaking residential projects that have sprouted up since the High Line's debut. While this neighborhood's zoning constraints limit the building's height to a mere seven stories comprising 53 apartment units, the building sets a cool yet bold tone with its bent metal formwork of charcoal-colored spandrels and oversized soundproof windows. The building's interior presents a purposely zen aesthetic with bamboo flooring, river-washed stone panels, and driftwood sculptural accents. One striking element on the building's rooftop, which may be seen from many points in the neighborhood, is the prominent sculpture *Perhaps* by Robert Buchholz.

DEVELOPER:

Centaur Properties

COMPLETED:

2008

THE BLUE TOWER

101 NORFOLK STREET, NEW YORK, NEW YORK

COLLABORATION, MIXED-USE, CONDOMINIUM, RETAIL

Located in Manhattan's Lower East Side, The Blue Tower was designed in collaboration with Bernard Tschumi Architects. Using zoning code as a generator of form, the building's massing is comprised of oblique angles which allow for setbacks and cantilevering volumes. These moves are a part of the strategy to accomplish a specific architectural statement within the confines of a tight budget and strict zoning regulations. The signature blue color stands in opposition to the neutral palette of the surrounding urban fabric, and the pixelated pattern on the façade responds to the varying program within. At 16 stories and 44,000 square feet, the building is comprised of 32 condominiums in addition to full retail space on the ground level.

EXECUTIVE ARCHITECT:
SLCE Architects

DESIGN ARCHITECT:
Bernard Tschumi Architects

DEVELOPER:
On the Level Design and Construction, LLC

COMPLETED:
2007

88 WASHINGTON PLACE

NEW YORK, NEW YORK

MARKET-RATE CONDOMINIUM

SLCE Architects has built a reputation for shepherding new designs through the New York City Landmarks Commission in contextually sensitive Landmark Districts. This new condominium at 88 Washington Place in New York had the additional structural challenge of resting partially above a subway tunnel.

DEVELOPER:

Development Consortium

COMPLETED:

2007

10 WEST END AVENUE

NEW YORK, NEW YORK

CONDOMINIUM

This site was part of a two-block manufacturing district, which had been underutilized for decades. SLCE worked with the Department of City Planning, land-use attorneys, and community groups to rezone this area into what became the vibrant Lincoln West neighborhood, just west of the Lincoln Center campus. 10 West End Avenue was the first of many buildings to break ground and filled a need for for-sale residences.

At 31 stories and 350,000 square feet, the building is comprised of 173 luxury condominiums ranging from one- to three-bedroom apartments, as well as seven penthouses.

The building's glass-clad façade permits 11-foot floor-to-ceiling windows, offering breathtaking views of the city as well as allowing ample natural light into rooms. Amenities include a 2,300-square-foot state-of-the-art fitness center, including a spa and 50-foot pool, as well as a 24-hour doorman and children's play area. 10 West End Avenue remains an important addition to this now-established neighborhood.

DEVELOPERS:

Cambridge Development

Apollo Real Estate Advisors

COMPLETED:

2007

Photo Credit: Corporate Photographics / Bob Zucker: Photographer

ELEMENT

555 WEST 59TH STREET, NEW YORK, NEW YORK

CONDOMINIUM

Element came to life as the result of a rezoning effort comprising the few blocks of an underutilized manufacturing district residing between Lincoln Center and the far West Side, now known as the Lincoln West neighborhood.

SLCE was the lead architect spearheading this rezoning, along with land-use attorneys, community groups, and the City Planning Commission, and resulted in numerous commissions for the firm, of which Element was the second. Element was able to achieve its 33-story height by virtue of its through-block site, which allowed its height, unusual for a mid-block site, to clear the rigid sky exposure planes requisite for this area.

Its 198 luxury condominium units reside in a rounded glass-cornered shaft, which embodies the aesthetic of a streamlined ocean liner gracing the New York City skyline along the Hudson River

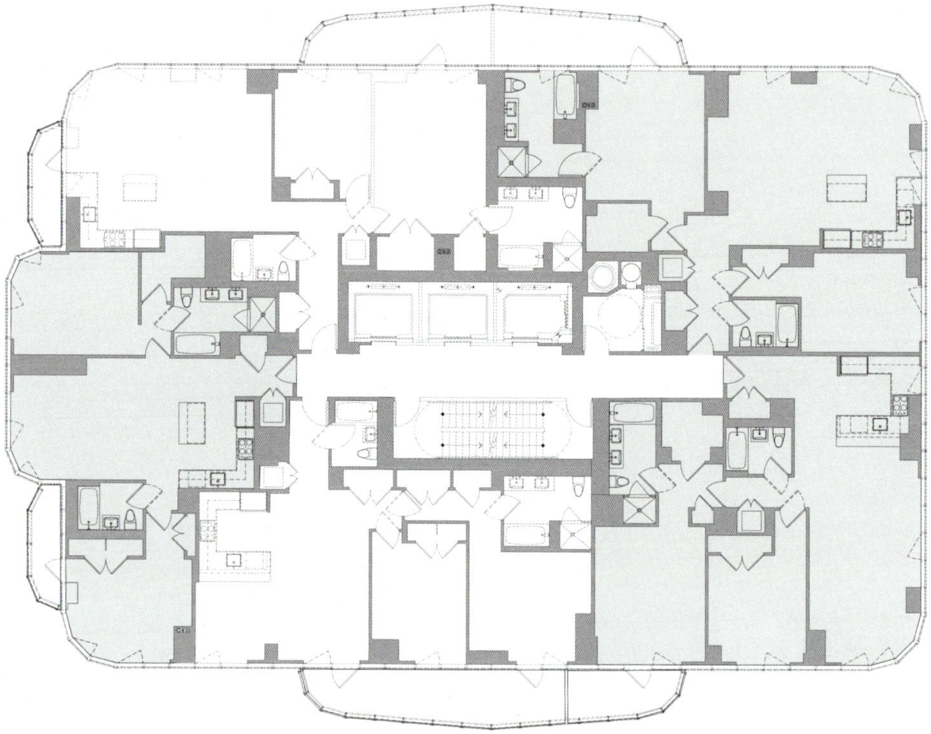

CALATRAVA

to the west. As is often the story with New York City development, the Hudson River views—as well as the dramatic skyline of the Upper West Side—were fast compromised by other major developments in subsequent years, but the building still holds its own among its peers.

Amenities include a private landscaped park, health club with enclosed pool, Studio Maestro dance school, and below-grade parking.

AWARD:

2007 Concrete Industry Board of New York Annual Award

DEVELOPER:

Continental Ventures

COMPLETED:

2007

40 MERCER STREET

NEW YORK, NEW YORK

COLLABORATION, MIXED-USE, CONDOMINIUM, RETAIL

Designed in collaboration with Ateliers Jean Nouvel, 40 Mercer Street is a 13-story, 160,000-square-foot condominium building featuring 40 luxury units. The building is situated on a former department store site located in the SoHo historic district in Lower Manhattan. Consistent with the neighborhood, the project includes retail and residential amenity spaces on the ground and basement levels.

The notable feature of the building is its very big windows, which comprise the entirety of the façade. A number of windows open with the push of a button, and the largest of them are 11 feet high by 20 feet long. A series of terraces wrap around the building and feature swimming pools, a common outdoor area, and four outdoor cabanas. A unique keycard system at the lobby level identifies the unit owners and takes them directly to their floor.

BROADWAY
GRAND ST

AWARDS:

2008 Engineering News-Record (ENR) Magazine, Best of the Best Awards: Best Residential Project

New York Construction News Best of 2008 Awards: Project of the Year (High-Rise Residential)

EXECUTIVE ARCHITECT:

SLCE Architects

DESIGN ARCHITECT:

Ateliers Jean Nouvel

DEVELOPERS:

Hines

Whitehall

COMPLETED:

2007

37

ECHELON CHELSEA

35 WEST 21ST STREET, NEW YORK, NEW YORK

REHABILITATION, MIXED-USE RESIDENTIAL

Echelon Chelsea is located in the Ladies' Mile historic district and is subject to the NYC Landmarks Preservation Commission's strict design review and approval process. SLCE's design illustrates the firm's growing acceptance within the design community and among preservationists and community groups for superior design. The through-block site allows for different design solutions for each street frontage. The major building component, which fronts West 21st Street, is organized in a tripartite composition, both horizontally in a symmetrical bookended fashion and vertically in a base, shaft, and crown configuration, which was the accepted design convention of the fin-de-siècle era.

DEVELOPER:

Roseland Management

COMPLETED:

2007

100, 120 & 140 RIVERSIDE BOULEVARD

NEW YORK, NEW YORK

MIXED-USE, LUXURY CONDOMINIUM, MARKET-RATE RENTAL

After many false starts and much community opposition to a mixed-use development built over exposed Grand Central railroad tracks, developers received consent for 16 residential buildings of varying height in the late 1980s for this stretch of Riverside Boulevard. SLCE garnered commissions for the three buildings centered on the overall development—100, 120, and 140 Riverside Boulevard. Working in concert with community groups, the Department of City Planning, and the Municipal Arts Society, these three buildings, being in the center of the larger development, managed the transition from the more masonry-clad aesthetic associated with prewar Riverside Drive to the north and the more reflective window and curtain-wall buildings—that identify more with the burgeoning Midtown aesthetic—to its south. Hudson River views were maximized and the buildings' color palettes varied with each building's distinct personality. 140 was designed as a market-rate rental scheme, and 100 and 120 were designed for the luxury for-sale market.

DEVELOPERS:

New World Development

The Trump Organization

Extell Development Company

COMPLETED:

2002–2007

700 GROVE STREET

JERSEY CITY, NEW JERSEY

CONDOMINIUM

Located on the border of Hoboken and Jersey City, this 12-story, 331,000-square-foot condominium is comprised of 230 studios and one- and two-bedroom units. Parking and amenity spaces are accommodated within the building. An exterior amenity space and plaza area was constructed as a green roof over the parking structure.

The building was constructed using reinforced concrete flat plates, and features both punched windows and a window-wall system. This was one of SLCE's first buildings to utilize insulation inside of the exterior cavity of the building, behind the brick veneer façade that begins above the first floor. Cast stone completes the façade of the building beneath the brick veneer.

DEVELOPER:
Toll Brothers City Living

COMPLETED:
2005

THE VERDESIAN

211 NORTH END AVENUE, NEW YORK, NEW YORK

COLLABORATION, MARKET-RATE RENTAL

Located in Battery Park City, The Verdesian is a 24-story, market-rate rental tower containing 253 energy-efficient apartments. The Verdesian is the first residential high-rise to attain a Platinum LEED rating, the highest ranking for sustainable design from the U.S. Green Building Council. In the same neighborhood, The Solaire, also designed by Pelli Clarke Pelli Architects and developed by The Albanese Organization, was the world's first green residential high-rise building, for which SLCE provided executive architect services, zoning expertise, and residential planning guidance.

Building amenities include a 24-hour concierge service, a landscaped roof terrace, children's playroom, fitness center, and on-site parking with electric vehicle charging stations.

EXECUTIVE ARCHITECT:

SLCE Architects

DESIGN ARCHITECT:

Pelli Clarke Pelli Architects

DEVELOPER:

The Albanese Organization

COMPLETED:

2006

THREE TEN

310 EAST 53RD STREET, NEW YORK, NEW YORK

COLLABORATION, CONDOMINIUM

Three Ten is located at the southeast corner of East 53rd Street and Second Avenue on the Upper East Side of Manhattan. Noticeable for its elegant combination of a stone base and a 30-story glazed tower with balconies integrated into its exterior wall system, it is a luxury full-service condo with a doorman, concierge, gym, laundry room, courtyard, on-site garage, and bicycle storage.

The 88 residences at Three Ten are comprised of three distinct types of apartments: Tower Residences, with a continuous floor-to-ceiling window wall; open-plan Duplex Residences, with double-height ceilings and windows; and two private Mansion Residences, each with 4,000 square feet of living area. The building also features a garden, storage, and retail on the Second Avenue frontage.

EXECUTIVE ARCHITECT:

SLCE Architects

DESIGN ARCHITECTS FOR THE ENVELOPE:

MdeAS Architects

ARC

DEVELOPER:

Macklowe Properties

COMPLETED:

2005

THE MARBELLA & M2

425 WASHINGTON BOULEVARD, JERSEY CITY, NEW JERSEY
MARKET-RATE HOUSING

Located along the main waterfront thoroughfare of Washington Boulevard in Jersey City, this full-block site was originally envisioned as a phased development comprising two 40-story residential towers linked by a shared parking structure, with a landscaped deck benefiting all residents. The superstructure for the second building, including pilings, was built into the first phase in anticipation of a full build-out. As it turned out—for various market reasons—while the first phase was completed in 2004, the second phase was not completed until 2016. Each tower was designed to complement the other, but the second tower, branded M2, presents a more contemporary lifestyle both in the building's exterior design and its interior finishes. The buildings' many amenities include an outdoor landscaped pool and a full complement of indoor fitness and club rooms.

DEVELOPER:
Roseland Residential Trust

COMPLETED:
2004 and 2016

MILAN

300 EAST 55TH STREET,
NEW YORK, NEW YORK
CONDOMINIUM

Completed in 2004, Milan was one of the first of a growing number of residential buildings along this section of Third Avenue in the East 50s to be entirely rendered in window wall. The building's chamfers lend a lean verticality to the tower, which contrasts with its older neighbors typically rendered in brick masonry.

The Milan's 152 apartments addressed the need for larger-proportioned units and a higher level of finish than this neighborhood ordinarily produced, and included a high-end appliance package, cherry-wood flooring, landscaped garden, full-service garage, club room, and health club.

DEVELOPER:
Worldwide Holdings
COMPLETED:
2005

“SLCE, THOUGH THE MOST PROLIFIC, IS ALSO PERHAPS AMONG THE MOST DISCREET. THE FIRM IS LINKED TO SOME OF THE MOST PROMINENT RESIDENTIAL DEVELOPMENTS IN THE CITY, BUT ITS NAME IS OFTEN OBSCURED IN THE SHADOW OF A FLASHY INTERNATIONAL STARCHITECT.”

Kathryn Brenzel, “Who’s Designing NYC’s Skyline?” *The Real Deal,* March 2018

CHELSEA TOWER

100 WEST 26TH STREET, NEW YORK, NEW YORK

MIXED-USE, RESIDENTIAL, RETAIL

Built in 2003, Chelsea Tower, the second project to be designed along the Sixth Avenue corridor by SLCE under a revised zoning ordinance, comprises 34 stories. It is situated in the Flower District of Chelsea, only a modest portion of which yet exists. The distinguishing elements of this "Tower on a Base" include lovely plum-colored brick piers flanking vertical shafts of floor-to-ceiling glass set in statuary bronze-anodized frames. SLCE not only designed the exterior, but also provided interior design services, presenting a hip Midtown aesthetic which has held up well since its opening in an increasingly competitive rental market. The building contains 228 apartments ranging from studios to two-bedrooms. Resident amenities include a 2,500-square-foot landscaped roof, fitness center, laundry facility, on-site parking garage, resident manager and valet services, and a healthy component of neighborhood ground-floor retail uses.

DEVELOPERS:

Steinberg & Pokoik

The DeMatteis Organization

COMPLETED:

2003

PAR

KOFFEECAKE CORNER
COFFEE • BAKERY • DESSERT

THE ATLAS

66 WEST 38TH STREET, NEW YORK, NEW YORK

MIXED-USE, RESIDENTIAL, OFFICE BUILDING, RETAIL BASE

At 47 stories and 390,000 square feet, The Atlas comprises 374 rental units atop ground-floor retail, four stories of commercial office space, and below-grade accessory parking.

The Atlas takes its design cues from the Art Deco commercial office building neighborhood in which it presently resides. Its limestone base is topped with the building's cascading form, while the tower's vertical piers reach to the sky with rooftop finial flourishes. It's only since the 1990s that developers have braved this part of lower Midtown with major residential buildings, providing more of a 24/7 environment. Since that time, SLCE has designed dozens of residential towers in this relatively new mixed-use neighborhood that was historically associated with the fashion industry.

DEVELOPER:
Gotham Organization

COMPLETED:
2002

THE BILTMORE

270 WEST 47TH STREET, NEW YORK, NEW YORK

MIXED-USE, RESIDENTIAL, OFFICE BUILDING, RETAIL

This 51-story, 445,000-square-foot luxury building is located in the heart of the Theater District. The Biltmore comprises 464 residential units, a lounge and health club, retail space on the first floor, and office space on the second and third floors. The building gets its name through the vehicle of Theater Rehabilitation—a credit derived from the adjacent landmarked Biltmore Theatre—in return for additional floor area. The tapering tower shaft sports an angled projection that recalls the angle of Broadway (a block away), as well as vestiges of a preexisting stream which ran through the property prior to the superposition of the Manhattan street grid.

DEVELOPERS:

The Jack Parker Organization

The Moinian Group

COMPLETED:

2003

THE METROPOLIS

150 EAST 44TH STREET,
NEW YORK, NEW YORK

MIXED-USE, MARKET-RATE RESIDENTIAL, RETAIL

The Metropolis, completed in 2002, represented a willingness on the part of residential developers to construct major residential towers set squarely in the heart of this solidly Midtown commercial office environment, located close to major transit hubs such as Grand Central Station, which is located a mere half block away to the west across Lexington Avenue. SLCE garnered this commission as the result of a limited competition organized by the developer, resulting in this gleaming residential tower highlighted by a major bow that runs up the entire 48-story shaft, culminating at its crown with a roof terrace accessible to all residents. The Metropolis's 361 apartment units, street-oriented retail, health club, and other amenities are all housed within 356,000 square feet of floor area.

AWARD:
Award of Merit, The Concrete Industry Board of New York

DEVELOPER:
Rose Associates

COMPLETED:
2002

101 WEST END AVENUE

NEW YORK, NEW YORK

MIXED-USE, CONDOMINIUM, RETAIL

101 West End Avenue's twin tower design, coupled with extensive use of silver-framed, floor-to-ceiling glass and piers of sandstone-hued brick, recalls the modernist trends of the prewar era found in Art Deco buildings such as The Century. An active streetscape is assured by a retail base, and the dual towers are crowned by lit lanterns that further distinguish this building from its neighbors. A full complement of amenities provided at 101 West End Avenue continues this neighborhood trend. At 33 stories and 750,000 square feet, the building is comprised of 507 luxury apartment units, a parking garage, retail space, and a health club, among other amenities.

AWARD:
Best of 2000 Award, New York Construction News

DEVELOPER:
Tishman Speyer

COMPLETED:
2000

AVALON WILLOW

746 MAMARONECK AVENUE,
MAMARONECK, NEW YORK

MARKET-RATE RENTAL

The Avalon Willow is a rental apartment building located near Metro-North's Mamaroneck station in Westchester County, New York. The 258,000-square-foot project consists of 227 residential units in three four-story clusters which wrap around a landscaped recreation area and swimming pool, all atop a 379-car parking facility. Other amenities include a health club and resident lounge. The building features pitched roofs, and brick and stucco façades.

AWARD:
2000 Westchester American Institute of Architects Community Design Award

DEVELOPER:
AvalonBay Communities

COMPLETED:
2000

MADISON BELVEDERE

10 EAST 29TH STREET,
NEW YORK, NEW YORK
MARKET RATE HOUSING

DEVELOPER:
Rose Associates
COMPLETED:
1999

Rose Associates was the pioneering developer of Madison Belvedere, which was at the forefront of the renewal of this overlooked part of South Midtown. Though centrally located, the area had been in varying stages of decay for decades. Upon the completion of this finely detailed, rose-toned, 48-story residential tower comprising 404 luxury apartments and a health club, an array of restaurants and services sprang up nearby and led to further development in what is now a vibrant neighborhood during all hours of the day. The building's distinctive crown is lit in the evening, imparting Madison Belvedere with a stature that proclaims the renaissance of this revitalized neighborhood.

THE AVALON BRONXVILLE

125 PARKWAY ROAD, BRONXVILLE, NEW YORK

MARKET-RATE RENTAL HOUSING

The Avalon Bronxville is a new-construction, five-story residential building located in Bronxville, New York, adjacent to the Metro-North station. At 137,000 square feet, the building is comprised of 110 units and amenities including a recreation deck, health club, and tenant lounge. The discreet subterranean parking facility, pitched shingle roofs, and brick and stucco façades help the project blend with the scale and tone of the surrounding neighborhood.

DEVELOPER:

AvalonBay Communities

COMPLETED:

1999

THE VANGUARD

77 WEST 24TH STREET,
NEW YORK, NEW YORK
MIXED-USE, MARKET-RATE RENTAL, RETAIL

As a result of a 1995 zoning change converting a large area of Chelsea from manufacturing to mixed residential and commercial uses, the entire Sixth Avenue corridor running from 23rd to 34th Streets became ripe for extensive residential development, and assuming all the characteristics of a vital 24/7 mixed-use neighborhood. The Vanguard was the first SLCE-designed project of many to follow, developed as a mixed-use, multi-family rental apartment building, with an affordable component and a retail base. The building's 300 residences range from studios to two-bedrooms, and amenities include a 24-hour concierge, fitness center and landscaped roof terrace, and bicycle and tenant storage.

The Vanguard achieved Platinum LEED-EB certification through its green practices and conservation efforts during the design and construction phases.

Ultimately, SLCE designed six major towers along this now-vibrant avenue, of which few sites remain for future development.

DEVELOPER:
The Albanese Organization

COMPLETED:
1999

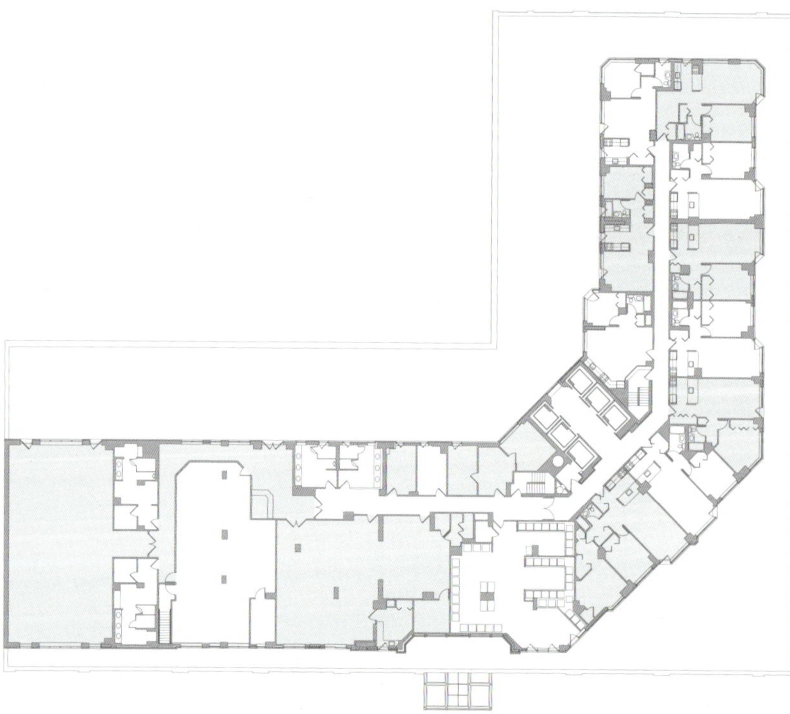

THE GERSHWIN

250 WEST 50TH STREET, NEW YORK, NEW YORK

MARKET-RATE RENTAL, RETAIL BASE

Located in the heart of the Theater District in Midtown, The Gershwin represents the close of an era where anything rental was required to be rendered in brick. Completed in 1998 and standing at 40 stories, the 550 market-rate rental apartments were a major residential addition to this district. Christened "The Gershwin" by the original developer, the building subsequently changed hands twice and is presently included in the extensive portfolio of AvalonBay Communities. Occupying the entire frontage along Eighth Avenue from 49th to 50th Streets, the building commands a major presence, which is refined by its undulating façade of bay windows and 50th Street corner prow. Retail frontage is uninterrupted along the avenue, and the residential entrance, dominated by a major bronze marquee, is located along the relatively quiet side street.

DEVELOPER:

Jack Resnick and Sons

COMPLETED:

1998

ONE UNION SQUARE SOUTH

NEW YORK, NEW YORK

COLLABORATION, MIXED-USE, RESIDENTIAL, COMMERCIAL, RETAIL

One Union Square, designed by Davis Brody Bond, is a distinctive building owing to its bold massing, red-brick masonry façade, and art installation on the north front known as *Metronome*, created by Kristen Jones and Andrew Ginzel. This particular block directly fronting Union Square had been deteriorating for decades, despite the large-scale development of Zeckendorf Towers directly to the east, erected a decade earlier. The developer's major commitment to this strategically located block proved essential to what has become a newly vibrant neighborhood and transportation hub.

At 27 stories and 174,000 square feet, the building is comprised of 240 units, ranging from luxury studios to one- and two-bedroom apartments. Amenities include a 24-hour concierge and doorman, health and fitness center, landscaped rooftop sun terrace, residents' barbecue terrace, and quarter-acre "great lawn," offering iconic views of Union Square's celebrated Green Market, Greenwich Village, and the Midtown skyline.

The retail base contains a large cineplex at the northeast corner of 13th Street and Broadway, while big-box retail space fronts this vibrant commercial 14th Street corridor.

SLCE provided executive architect services which included residential planning, zoning expertise, and technical services.

EXECUTIVE ARCHITECT:
SLCE Architects

DESIGN ARCHITECT:
Davis Brody Bond

DEVELOPER:
The Related Companies

COMPLETED:
1998

WELLINGTON TOWER

350 EAST 82ND STREET, NEW YORK, NEW YORK
COLLABORATION, CONDOMINIUM

Located in the relatively quiet Yorkville neighborhood of Manhattan's Upper East Side, Wellington Tower's brick, granite, and limestone façade recalls the Art Deco style of New York's grand era of residential construction of the 1920s. While originally built as a high-end rental building in 1999, the 18-story tower was converted to luxury condominiums in 2005.

Wellington Tower comprises 156 spacious residences, ranging from studios to five-bedroom apartments. Residents enjoy generously sized, light-filled apartments and superior amenities including an Olympic swimming pool, spa and fitness center, 24-hour doorman, and a cinema.

EXECUTIVE ARCHITECT:
SLCE Architects
DESIGN ARCHITECT:
Hartman-Cox Architects
DEVELOPER:
RFR Holding
COMPLETED:
1999

CITY LIGHTS

4–74 48TH AVENUE, LONG ISLAND CITY, NEW YORK

COLLABORATION, RESIDENTIAL, PUBLIC SCHOOL

In collaboration with Cesar Pelli and Associates, City Lights was the first of many buildings constructed at Queens West along the East River in Long Island City, Queens. City Lights is a majestic 42-story tower offering 521 remarkably affordable co-op apartments.

The building offers affordable luxury—an elegant lobby with 24-hour concierge, covered parking for over 500 cars, a residents-only health club, and tennis courts. It offers state-of-the-art communications with high-speed internet access, close-circuit security, and an advanced refuse recycling system. The building also houses a 350-seat K–5 public school.

EXECUTIVE ARCHITECT:
SLCE Architects
DESIGN ARCHITECT:
Cesar Pelli and Associates
DEVELOPERS:
Parcel 10 Associates
The Trotwood Corporation
COMPLETED:
1997

THE HELUX

520 WEST 43RD STREET, NEW YORK, NEW YORK

CONDOMINIUM

The newly branded Helux is a 34-story rental tower in New York's Hell's Kitchen. The building has a two-toned rose brick façade and a two-story limestone base fronting 43rd Street. There are 375 apartments in the building, ranging from studios to two-bedrooms. The particular zoning in what is referred to as the Perimeter Area of the Special Clinton District generated a huge amount of development flanking either side of West 42nd Street, resulting in rows of residential towers, many of which were designed by SLCE.

The on-site amenities include a 24-hour concierge, bicycle and tenant storage, lounge, playroom, fitness center with a basketball court and saunas, garage, and rooftop terrace.

DEVELOPER:
Gotham Organization

COMPLETED:
1996

300 EAST 64TH STREET

NEW YORK, NEW YORK

MARKET-RATE RESIDENTIAL

300 East 64th Street is an example of how a development site successfully deals with the city's "Tower on a Base" regulation. It also demonstrates SLCE's ability to integrate a new luxury 27-story residence of 101 units, new cinema, and retail space over an existing cinema—while in use—into a single unified composition. Extensive limestone trim and detailing at the base recall a prewar aesthetic typical of East Side luxury residences. Chamfered glass corners and inset bay windows at the tower add interest to the building's profile and set the product apart from the more conventional neighbors dating from the 1960s and 1970s.

AWARD:

1996 Award of Merit, The Concrete Industry Board of New York

DEVELOPER:

RFR Holding

COMPLETED:

1996

"WHILE MOST OF SLCE'S WORK—10.90 MILLION SQUARE FEET—WAS IN MANHATTAN, THE FIRM WAS ALSO THE MOST ACTIVE IN QUEENS DURING THE SIX-YEAR PERIOD WITH 5.22 MILLION SQUARE FEET IN THAT BOROUGH. AND THE FIRM ALSO RANKED NO. 3 IN BROOKLYN WITH 3.62 MILLION SQUARE FEET."

Kathryn Brenzel, "Who's Designing NYC's Skyline?" *The Real Deal*, March 2018

MILLENNIUM TOWER

101 WEST 67TH STREET, NEW YORK, NEW YORK

COLLABORATION, CONDOMINIUM

Built in 1994, Millennium Tower is a luxury condominium tower in Lincoln Square and is regarded as one of most prestigious residences in the area. The building was the most important mixed-use tower on the Upper West Side at the time of erection, containing a 12-screen movie theater, a post office, retail space, large Reebok health club, and 368 residences. Resident amenities include: 24-hour doorman and concierge service; special membership rates to the 117,000-square-foot Reebok Club, whose facilities include basketball courts, a running track, swimming pool, and rock-climbing wall; and a rooftop lounge. The building received LEED Gold certification.

EXECUTIVE ARCHITECT:
SLCE Architects
DESIGN ARCHITECT:
Kohn Pedersen Fox Associates
DEVELOPER:
Millennium Partners
COMPLETED:
1994

30 EAST 85TH STREET

NEW YORK, NEW YORK

CONDOMINIUM

A successful marriage between stringent height and setback requirements and the desire for a distinctively sculpted building, 30 East 85th Street positively contributes to the Upper East Side skyline by evoking the grand era of the New York prewar apartment building with its rusticated granite piers and cornices and salmon-colored Roman brick. At 31 stories, the building includes 98 family-sized units. The entrance lobby is off the side street, as is typical of an Upper East Side image, and the building is only a stone's throw from Central Park and Museum Mile.

DEVELOPER:

The Zucker Organization

COMPLETED:

1987

THE CORONADO

155 WEST 70TH STREET, NEW YORK, NEW YORK

CONDOMINIUM

Although not sited within the Upper West Side historic district at the time of its construction, The Coronado was designed with its context in mind. A sizeable corner bay window merging the side street with Broadway, Juliet balconies with wrought-iron balustrades, a fin-de-siècle entrance canopy flanked on either side by brooding sculptures, and special brick shapes which articulated the major building piers were all features which acknowledged this late 19th- and early 20th-century neighborhood. This building was also first in this neighborhood to adhere to Housing Quality (later renamed Quality Housing) standards, which mandated a maximum 210-foot building height and street wall (these standards were subsequently applied to many neighborhoods of varying densities within the five boroughs of the city). At 21 stories and 153,000 square feet, the building is comprised of 124 for-sale units, in addition to numerous amenities including a health club, pool, playroom, billiard room, and bicycle storage.

DEVELOPER:
Sherwood Equities

COMPLETED:
1990

THE FLEA

TRIBECA TOWER

105 DUANE STREET, NEW YORK, NEW YORK

MARKET-RATE RENTAL

Located in one of New York's oldest and most historic neighborhoods, Tribeca Tower rises 52 stories, making it the tallest and most distinctive building in the Tribeca area at the time of completion. The building's 451 apartments range from studios to two-bedrooms, offering floor-to-ceiling windows. Resident amenities include a stunning two-story attended lobby, designed by David Rockwell, with 24-hour concierge, doorman, valet, and laundry services, as well as an entertainment lounge, fitness center, and rooftop sun terrace.

AWARD:

1991 Build New York Award

DEVELOPER:

The DeMattis Organization,
subsequently Related Companies

COMPLETED:

1990

METROPOLITAN TOWER

146 WEST 57TH STREET, NEW YORK, NEW YORK

MIXED-USE, RESIDENTIAL, OFFICE BUILDING, RETAIL

Metropolitan Tower's sheer "frameless" glass façade and wedge-shaped form became an instantly recognized icon for high-end residential architecture. Its angular form orientates the largest portion of the apartments toward views of Central Park. Harry Macklowe provided the vision required to break the mold of conventional Manhattan residential development aesthetics in producing this design, which partner Peter Claman succeeded in realizing. The building's program also includes a large commercial office base, ground-floor retail, a residential amenities floor, and a parking garage. Upon its completion in 1986, this 650,000-square-foot property, comprised of 243 condominiums and office spaces, became the seventh-tallest concrete structure in New York.

DEVELOPER:

Macklowe Properties

COMPLETED:

1986

100 UNITED NATIONS PLAZA

NEW YORK, NEW YORK

MARKET-RATE CONDOMINIUM

100 United Nations Plaza's soaring vertical profile has become an East Side landmark. This 51-story glass and brick monolithic sculptural tower contains 267 luxury condominium apartments above the 11,400-square-foot public plaza, which conceals a 52-space parking facility. 100 United Nations Plaza was designed by Der Scutt Architects and SLCE worked as executive architect.

AWARD:

1985 Concrete Industry Board of New York Award for Exceptional Merit

EXECUTIVE ARCHITECT:

SLCE Architects

DESIGN ARCHITECT:

Der Scutt Architects

DEVELOPER:

The Albanese Organization

COMPLETED:

1987

STERLING PLAZA

255 EAST 49TH STREET, NEW YORK, NEW YORK

CONDOMINIUM

Sterling Plaza can easily be recognized on East 49th Street by its 33-story distinctive white-crowned rooftop on the northwest corner of Second Avenue. Designed in collaboration with Arquitectonica, the building is comprised of 176 apartments, many of which have balconies that define and strengthen the structure's corners. Amenities include a full-time doorman, concierge, and laundry services.

EXECUTIVE ARCHITECT:

SLCE Architects

DESIGN ARCHITECT:

Arquitectonica

DEVELOPER:

Sterling Equities

COMPLETED:

1982

45 WEST 67TH STREET

NEW YORK, NEW YORK

RESIDENTIAL CONDOMINIUM ON OFFICE BASE

45 West 67th Street was designed within the contextual guidelines of a "Tower on a Base," comprising six stories of neighborhood retail and office space originally for ABC television studios. The tower comprises 171 residential condominium units, with amenities that include a private garden courtyard and exercise room. The building's street wall meets the varying heights of its adjacent neighbors, six stories along Columbus Avenue and 13 stories along West 67th Street. The tower portion, set back from the street, reaches 33 stories. Red-colored Norman-sized brick seemed a natural color selection for this residential neighborhood, with limestone and marble finishing off the base. Recessed planters along the side street straddle a traditionally scaled residential lobby fronting leafy West 67th Street, with Central Park a short walk away.

DEVELOPER:

The Brodsky Organization

COMPLETED:

1983

"THE BRILLIANT WAY THE ARCHITECTS PLACED THE FOOTPRINT OF THE TOWER AT AN ANGLE LETS OUR TENANTS EXPERIENCE MANHATTAN'S SKYLINE FROM A UNIQUE PERSPECTIVE. SLCE ARCHITECTS CREATED A UNIQUE WORK OF ARCHITECTURE."

3

AFFORDABLE, SENIOR & SUPPORTIVE HOUSING

SUNRISE AT EAST 56TH STREET

139 EAST 56TH STREET,
NEW YORK, NEW YORK
ASSISTED LIVING

Located in Midtown Manhattan, 139 East 56th Street is a newly constructed assisted-living facility. At 17 stories and 130,000 square feet, the building is comprised of 151 units, in addition to 6,900 square feet of retail space at the ground level. The building's community spaces are located on the second floor, which feature floor-to-ceiling windows to allow for a sense of transparency within the neighborhood. The residential floors three through 16 are arranged by need. Memory care and assisted living occupy their own respective floors and feature their own specific accompanying spaces. Additional amenity space is scattered throughout these residential floors, creating micro-neighborhoods within the building. Landscaped terraces add to this sense of community for the residents.

The building is organized vertically, unlike most senior living communities. Inspired by classic Park Avenue apartment houses, its design and layout reflect New York City apartment living. This residence will set a new standard for senior housing and memory care, while proving to be an asset to the surrounding neighborhood.

DEVELOPERS:
Hines
REIT Welltower

EXPECTED COMPLETION:
2020

VAN DYKE III

405 DUMONT AVENUE, BROOKLYN, NEW YORK

AFFORDABLE HOUSING

Van Dyke III (formerly Dumont Commons) is a distinctive mixed-use affordable housing development situated within the Van Dyke Houses campus in Brooklyn's Brownsville neighborhood. At 12 stories and 205,500 square feet, the building is comprised of 188 apartments. The building also features a series of community facility spaces at the ground floor, making up 18,000 square feet of the total building area. This space provides a vital component to both the building tenants and the existing neighborhood residents in the form of an early childhood development center, a wellness center, and an urgent healthcare center. As part of the residential portion of the building, a supportive housing component will be included with service offices located on the ground floor. Residential amenities include a tenant recreation room, computer/library room, a fitness room, indoor bicycle parking, and landscaped exterior rear and roof terraces.

The building is designed as a concrete block and precast concrete plank superstructure sitting on a poured-in-place concrete pedestal base. The exterior envelope is a combination of architectural brick veneer construction with accents of aluminum composite metal paneling, along with both window-wall and punch-window glazing. High energy efficiency abounds in Van Dyke III in the form of Energy Star appliances and lighting fixtures, highly efficient heating and cooling systems, and eco-friendly interior finishes. Photovoltaic solar and solar thermal systems are also featured.

DEVELOPER:

Trinity Financial, Inc.

EXPECTED COMPLETION:

2021

SCHOOL BUS

THE WILFRID

1880 BATHGATE AVENUE, BRONX, NEW YORK

AFFORDABLE HOUSING

The Wilfrid will transform a former door manufacturing site to a mixed-use building with two eight-story residential towers. The project will total 225,000 square feet with 190 affordable apartment units ranging from 40 percent to 90 percent average median income, with several units with on-site office space. The base of the building will include a cellar parking garage, ground-floor retail of 23,000 square feet, and community facility space of 2,500 square feet. Building amenities will include resident lounges and laundry rooms in each tower, as well as a shared landscaped roof terrace and fitness room.

DEVELOPER:

Wilfred Realty Corp.

EXPECTED COMPLETION:

2019

1880 BOSTON ROAD

BRONX, NEW YORK
SENIOR HOUSING

1880 Boston Road, located in the West Farms neighborhood in the Bronx, is one of the first buildings to be developed as an Affordable Independent Residence for Seniors (AIRS) under Zoning for Quality and Affordability (ZQA). At nine stories, the building will have an area of 106,000 square feet

Under the new zoning resolution, there is no parking requirement for AIRS buildings located within the New York City transit zone. This allowed the project to be built in its entirety, due to the fact that it is a new tower being constructed on top of an existing two-story community center. The building will house 167 senior apartments in addition to the second-floor amenities, which include a yoga room, community room, art studio, library, and a rooftop terrace.

The building will be constructed using precast plank and prefabricated load-bearing exterior panels. The exterior façade will be composed of brick, metal, and corrugated panels in an effort to speak to the existing base building.

DEVELOPERS:

Foxy Management, Ltd.

Alembic Community Development

The Hebrew Home by RiverSpring Health

EXPECTED COMPLETION:

2018

MARKHAM GARDENS MANOR

1440 RICHMOND TERRACE, STATEN ISLAND, NEW YORK

SENIOR HOUSING

DEVELOPER:
Sisters of Charity

COMPLETED:
2013

Markham Gardens Manor was the final component of the Markham Gardens Development located in Staten Island's West Brighton neighborhood. The building was designated for funding under the United States Department of Housing and Urban Development Section 202 program for low-income senior citizens over the age of 62, and qualified as nonprofit housing for the elderly. The five-story, 60,000-square-foot building contains 80 dwelling units and is sited parallel to Richmond Terrace.

The building is comprised of 79 one-bedroom units for seniors, and a superintendent's unit. At the first-floor level, a community room with warming kitchen, library, computer room, laundry room, and ten apartments are provided. A partial basement houses mechanical rooms, tenant and building storage, an arts and crafts room, lounge, superintendent's office, and compactor. Each typical residential floor contains 17 one-bedroom senior units, along with a refuse room, compactor chute, and janitor's closet. The building features two egress stairs and two elevators, which operate without machine rooms. The site was landscaped and a passive outdoor recreation space was provided for residents. The site has gated access to the adjacent Markham Gardens Development, including the existing Markham Gardens Community Center, located on North Burgher Avenue.

Markham Gardens Manor was designed as a masonry building with a brick chosen to harmonize with the surrounding buildings. Universal design was incorporated into the construction to make the building readily usable by residents and visitors alike. Load-bearing masonry construction with precast concrete plank floors was utilized for the structure of the building. Double-hung, double-glazed aluminum windows with low e-glass were used. Through-wall air-conditioning sleeves with architectural louvers are located in each bedroom and living room.

Five percent of the units were designed for handicapped people and two percent of the units for the visually and hearing impaired. All units are handicap accessible and comply with Uniform Federal Accessibility Standard and New York City Local Law number 58/87. All areas of the building are also accessible, with adaptability and usage for all disabled visitors. The building is designed to accommodate aging in-place seniors. Grab bars in bathrooms, handrails in corridors, and nonslip materials on floors are provided to assist the elderly residents. In addition, an emergency pull-cord system is provided in the bathrooms and bedrooms of each unit.

ARTSBRIDGE

1450 PLIMPTON AVENUE, BRONX, NEW YORK

SENIOR HOUSING

ArtsBridge is a newly constructed masonry building for seniors built and funded by the Department of Housing and Urban Development under the HUD202 program. This seven-story, 78,400-square-foot building houses 62 affordable senior apartments along with a 21,400-square-foot community facility space located on the first floor, basement, and part of the second floor. The space will house nonprofit organizations who embrace a holistic approach to building communities and empowering residents—a philosophy adopted by the project's developer, Highbridge Community Development Corporation. An additional amenity of a large community room, library, and computer facilities occupies the building's seventh floor.

The apartments are expressed as a strong masonry element on the street corner, with punched windows in the dark brick façade. The lower two stories are cut back at the corner to expose the curtain wall, with Y-shaped columns supporting the upper floors.

DEVELOPER:
Highbridge HDFC

COMPLETED:
2017

MARCY SHERIDAN APARTMENTS

201 MARCY PLACE, BRONX, NEW YORK

AFFORDABLE HOUSING

Marcy Sheridan Apartments is a 71,604-square-foot, nine-story affordable housing development with 74 units and amenity spaces including a landscaped rear yard, an indoor recreation room, a library/computer room, an exercise room, a community room with a kitchen, and an on-premises laundry facility. The building has an on-site social services office providing supportive care to the residents. In addition, eight units are fully adapted to accommodate people with mobility difficulties; another four are adapted for people with visual or hearing impairments.

DEVELOPER:
Dunn Development Corp.

COMPLETED:
2016

HENRY PHIPPS PLAZA

325 EAST 25TH STREET, NEW YORK, NEW YORK

AFFORDABLE HOUSING

325 East 25th Street is a new-construction, nine-story apartment building located in Kips Bay. The 60,000-square-foot building features 56 units ranging from studios to three-bedrooms and which are split between middle-income and low-income households. A laundry room and community room are located on the first floor, and the rear yard features an outdoor passive recreation area. Rents at 325 East 25th Street are not to exceed a third of annual household income. The project is part of a larger scheme to renovate Phipps Houses, an affordable complex along 28th and 29th Streets.

DEVELOPER:
Phipps Houses

COMPLETED:
2016

BERGEN

BERGEN SARATOGA

331 SARATOGA AVENUE,
BROOKLYN, NEW YORK

AFFORDABLE HOUSING

Located in Brooklyn's Brownsville neighborhood, Bergen Saratoga Apartments is a five-story, 73,000-square-foot building comprised of 80 affordable housing units for low-income working families at 50 percent and 60 percent of area median income, along with units set aside for formerly homeless individuals under the New York III initiative. Space for dedicated supportive services is found on the first floor. Amenities include a community room with a kitchen, a library/computer room, a tenant garden, and a children's play area. The building also features a 24/7 front desk and there is off-street parking for 15 cars, along with indoor bicycle parking. This project is a true public-private partnership, with land contributed by the City of New York coupled with subsidies provided by the State of New York and private bank financing.

The building was constructed using insulated concrete forms (ICFs), which provide a continuously insulated cast-in-place concrete structure that significantly enhances thermal efficiency and performance when compared to traditional concrete masonry units (CMUs) or cast-in-place structures. Other green features include micro co-generation, Energy Star appliances, and energy-efficient LED lighting fixtures.

DEVELOPER:

Dunn Development Corp.

COMPLETED:

2016

LIVONIA COMMONS

LIVONIA AVENUE BETWEEN PENNSYLVANIA AVENUE & WILLIAMS AVENUE, BROOKLYN, NEW YORK

AFFORDABLE HOUSING

Located in the East New York neighborhood of Brooklyn, Livonia Commons seeks to revitalize the Livonia Avenue corridor with a dynamic mix of new affordable housing, retail stores, and community spaces. The building is comprised of 278 affordable housing units spanning four buildings and 277,000 square feet. The building serves families with a range of incomes, with more than half of the units dedicated for households earning less than 40 percent and 50 percent of area median income. Integrated into the project are 51 units of supportive housing with additional on-site support services.

In addition to meeting the needs of affordable housing in the neighborhood, Livonia Commons features 28,000 square feet of new retail stores and community space along with a new community arts center operated by Arts East New York.

The four buildings feature a traditional concrete block and precast concrete plank superstructure sitting on a steel frame pedestal base. The playful choice of color and interlocking shapes of brick and metal panel cladding enhance the vibrancy along the elevated subway corridor. The gradual step-down of the building's mass from the corner and away from the elevated subway tracks begins to break down the scale of the buildings and relates to the existing scale of the side streets.

All four buildings feature micro-generation and high-performance building systems, fixtures, and energy-efficient appliances.

AWARD:

2017 Building Brooklyn Award for affordable residential development

DEVELOPER:

Dunn Development Corp.

COMPLETED:

2016

CITY
SPEED
LIMIT
25
PHOTO
ENFORCED

SUGAR HILL HOUSING

410 WEST 155TH STREET, NEW YORK, NEW YORK

COLLABORATION, AFFORDABLE HOUSING

In collaboration with Adjaye Associates, this LEED Silver new-construction 13-story building features 171,000 square feet and 124 affordable housing rental apartments in a mix that ranges from studios to three-bedroom units. A precast graphite façade with rose prints wraps the building in a sawtooth pattern, which is evocative of the neighborhood's traditional row houses. The alternating pattern of the thermally broken windows provides ample light and air.

A 150-child day-care center occupies the ground level. Surrounding it is a clear acoustic glass storefront on all four faces of the building; residents also have access to an interior recreational courtyard. Eight classrooms, administrative offices, and a commercial kitchen complete this level.

Sugar Hill also houses a 16,000-square-foot children's museum for art and storytelling that resides mostly underground. High ceilings allow natural light to flood the space from a 60-foot skylight. Polished concrete floors, extensive wood paneling, and acoustic baffles welcome visitors to the three main galleries and the workshop classrooms. Not-for-profit office fronts on West 155th Street and a parking garage complete the program for this development.

All tenants have access to a ninth-floor community room and a roof terrace vegetable garden, as well as the main entry landscaped plaza.

AWARD:

2016 American Institute of Architects Design Awards: Merit Award

EXECUTIVE ARCHITECT:

SLCE Architects

DESIGN ARCHITECT:

Adjaye Associates

DEVELOPER:

Broadway Housing Communities

COMPLETED:

2014

KING GARDENS

211 RIVERDALE AVENUE,
BROOKLYN, NEW YORK

SENIOR HOUSING

King Gardens is a new-construction low-income senior housing apartment building developed in Brooklyn's Brownsville neighborhood.

At six stories and 52,000 square feet, the building includes 65 rental units and one superintendent's unit. All rental units serve low-income elderly families or elderly persons and developmentally disabled adults with incomes at or below 50 percent of the average median income of New York City. Rent for all units is subsidized by project-based Section 8 vouchers provided by New York State Homes and Community Renewal, and New York City Housing, Preservation and Development.

The building includes a large community room with kitchen, a laundry room for residents, supportive services office space, a library/computer room, resident activity rooms, and a landscaped rear yard. The building is designed to achieve Energy Star certification and incorporates extensive high-performance and energy-efficient components.

DEVELOPERS:

Dunn Development Corp.

Federation of Multicultural Programs, Inc.

COMPLETED:

2014

211
LIFT
PLOW
BLADE

THE PARK CLINTON

535 WEST 52ND STREET, NEW YORK, NEW YORK

AFFORDABLE HOUSING

The Park Clinton, located in Midtown Manhattan, is a 12-story, 100,000-square-foot cooperative living building comprised of 96 affordable housing units. Building amenities include a landscaped rear yard, fitness room, and indoor bicycle parking. All apartments feature modern, sustainable finishes and energy-efficient appliances.

The building is constructed of a steel frame and precast concrete plank superstructure, and features a prefabricated exterior envelope comprised of brick and metal panel cladding. Alluding to the contextual language of the old warehouse-style buildings found in the surrounding neighborhood, the building features a two-story ground base articulation, an emphasis on verticality for the bulk floors, and a top floor with rusticated brick articulation and a heavy cast-stone cornice.

DEVELOPERS:

Monadnock Development

Clinton Housing Association

COMPLETED:

2013

PUTNAM COURT

40 PUTNAM AVENUE, BROOKLYN, NEW YORK

AFFORDABLE HOUSING

Situated on a traditional brownstone block in the rapidly developing Clinton Hill neighborhood in Brooklyn, Putnam Court provides supportive housing for 34 formerly homeless adults along with affordable housing for 24 households earning up to 50 percent of area median income. At seven stories and 45,000 square feet, the building is comprised of 59 studio apartments. Amenity spaces include a landscaped rear terrace, community room, computer room and library, tenant storage, and on-site supportive services.

The masonry building has a concrete block and precast concrete plank superstructure, and features brick cladding and a broken-up façade, speaking to the nature of the surrounding brownstones. Putnam Court utilizes high-performance building systems and energy-efficient fixtures and appliances.

AWARD:
2014 NYC Big Apple Brownfield Award for the affordable housing category

DEVELOPER:
Dunn Development Corp.

COMPLETED:
2013

HIGHBRIDGE TERRACE & OVERLOOK

220–240 WEST 167TH STREET, BRONX, NEW YORK

AFFORDABLE HOUSING

Located along the Harlem River and Highbridge Park in the South Bronx, Highbridge Terrace and Overlook are two new-construction, low-income housing apartment buildings. The site was developed on vacant land purchased from the New York City Housing Authority (NYCHA) as part of joint efforts between it and Housing Preservation & Development to identify sites for affordable housing.

Rock outcrops and a steep slope added new challenges to the site, located on an underutilized corner, while considerations were made for the existing wooded area that serves the surrounding community. The final design features carefully thought-out foundations to achieve minimal site remediation. Outdoor terrace spaces are located on the roofs of the buildings in order to retain existing flora and take advantage of the sweeping views of Manhattan. The two buildings activate a long-vacant corner and promote pedestrian activity while bringing safety and security to residents of the community.

Highbridge Terrace, completed in 2010, is a seven-story, 67,900-square-foot building comprised of 65 units. Highbridge Overlook, completed in 2012, is an 11-story, 156,000-square-foot building comprised of 155 units. The 220 total units include studios and one-, two-, and three-bedroom apartments. The buildings provide affordable housing for low-income working families at 50 percent and 60 percent of area median income.

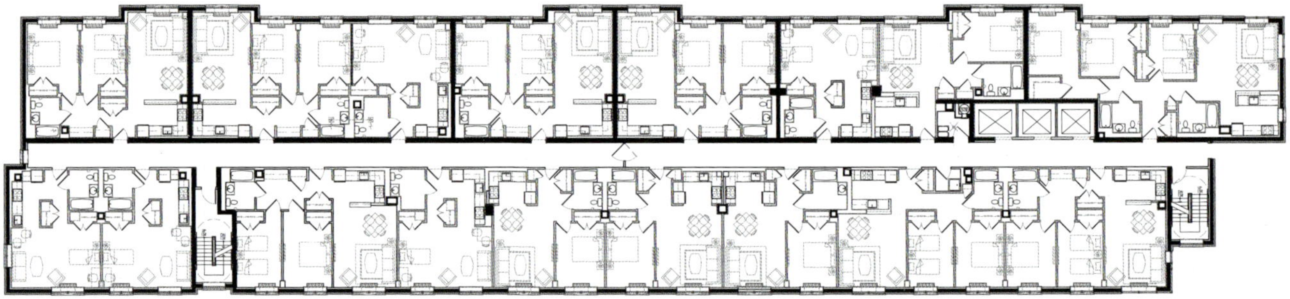

Highbridge Overlook 4th–9th floor plan (top), Highbridge Terrace 3rd–6th floor plan (bottom)

Additional units are set aside for formerly homeless families and for NYCHA residents.

Because of the unique topography of the site, all four façades of the buildings are quite visible. Varying tones of red and gray brick are featured on both buildings, with the use of metal panels as a unifying element. The buildings are designed to achieve Energy Star certification and incorporate extensive high-performance and energy-efficient components. Photovoltaic solar panels were installed on the main roof of Highbridge Overlook. Both buildings feature rooftop exterior terraces overlooking the East River, and many additional amenities. These include indoor recreation, community rooms, a computer room, on-site laundry, bicycle parking, and a covered parking garage.

DEVELOPER:

Dunn Development Corp.

COMPLETED:

2012

LEGACY & WESTWIND HOUSES

2081 MADISON AVENUE & 45 EAST 131ST STREET, NEW YORK, NEW YORK

AFFORDABLE HOUSING

Located in East Harlem in Manhattan, the Legacy and Westwind Houses are comprised of two eight-story buildings, providing a mix of supportive and affordable housing apartments with a total of 112 units spread over 110,000 square feet of building area. A number of apartments are set aside for formerly homeless singles, and Legacy Houses features a social services office at the ground floor, providing on-site services to the building tenants.

The buildings were designed to achieve Energy Star certification and feature various sustainable elements including eco-conscious interior finishes, LED lighting, and sustainably sourced wood flooring. Tenant amenities consist of interior recreation and community rooms, extensive landscaped rear gardens, a children's playground, and picnic areas shared by both buildings.

DEVELOPER:
Dunn Development Corp.

COMPLETED:
2012

WARBURTON RIVERVIEW

49 NORTH BROADWAY, YONKERS, NEW YORK

AFFORDABLE HOUSING

Warburton Riverview is a new-construction affordable housing building located in Yonkers, New York. At 12 stories and 67,000 square feet, the building is comprised of 74 affordable housing units. This building, along with five existing historic buildings on Warburton Avenue, is part of the revitalization of downtown Yonkers. The Warburton has a loading dock and parking on the lower level along with community spaces for the residents. A cast-in-place concrete base with load-bearing masonry and precast concrete plank forms the second floor through the roof level. The façade features two brick colors – the light brick accentuates the base and top of the building while darker red brick fills in the body of the building. Apartments facing Warburton Avenue have views of the scenic Hudson River and the adjacent waterfront developments.

DEVELOPER:
L&M Development Partners

COMPLETED:
2012

LAFAYETTE MANOR

226 FILLMORE STREET,
STATEN ISLAND, NEW YORK
SENIOR HOUSING

Lafayette Manor, located on the north shore of Staten Island, is a new-construction senior housing facility. The building was designated for funding under the U.S. Department of Housing and Urban Development Section 202 program for low-income senior citizens over the age of 62, and qualified as nonprofit housing for the elderly. As requested by the community board, the five-story, 50,000-square-foot building was designed to replicate the demolished Brighton City Hall. This design aspect was achieved with an 11-foot-high mansard roof, which envelops the entire fifth floor.

The building contains 24 studios and 35 one-bedroom units for seniors, along with a superintendent's unit. At the first-floor level, a community room with warming kitchen, library, computer room, arts and crafts room, and laundry room are provided. A partial basement houses mechanical rooms, and tenant and building storage. Each typical residential floor is comprised of 13 units, along with a refuse room, compactor chute, and janitor's closet. The building has two egress stairs and two elevators. The site was landscaped and a passive outdoor recreation space was provided for residents.

DEVELOPER:
Sisters of Charity of St. Vincent de Paul

COMPLETED:
2012

1710 VYSE AVENUE

BRONX, NEW YORK

SUPPORTIVE HOUSING

1710 Vyse Avenue is a five-story-with-basement supportive housing building funded by the State of New York's Office for Mental Health. The building has 65 dwelling units over 40,920 square feet, and auxiliary community facility spaces, social services offices, and an outdoor landscaped passive recreation space.

Community Access, sponsor of the project, is a pioneer in supportive housing and social services; promoting human rights, social justice, and economic opportunities. This project was its first community residence/single-room occupancy building.

SPONSOR:
Community Access

COMPLETED:
2011

DOUGLASS PARK, THE BALTON & ST. NICHOLAS PARK APARTMENTS

300 WEST 128TH STREET, 311 WEST 127TH STREET,
& 306 WEST 128TH STREET, NEW YORK, NEW YORK

AFFORDABLE HOUSING

These three buildings, although built at different times over the course of several years, are actually part of the same single-block assemblage in Harlem bounded by St. Nicholas Avenue, Frederick Douglass Boulevard, and West 127th and 128th Streets. SLCE, in consultation with the Department of City Planning and community groups, was able to upzone the entire block for a combination of market-rate and affordable housing. The red-brick palette speaks to the neighborhood's significant restoration efforts within a much larger area of resurgent Harlem. Upon completion in 2011, the entire development comprised 241 apartments and amenities within a total of 287,000 square feet of construction, and includes 125 accessory parking spaces concealed beneath a landscaped yard.

DEVELOPER:
The Richman Group

COMPLETED:
2011

LIBERTY AVENUE APARTMENTS

119 FOUNTAIN AVENUE, BROOKLYN, NEW YORK

AFFORDABLE HOUSING

This affordable housing project contains 43 units for both working families and adults with developmental disabilities. Seven apartments are fully accessible to people with disabilities: five for those with mobility difficulties, and two for those with hearing or vision impairments. In addition, all units are easily adaptable for persons with hearing, visual, or mobility impairments, and all public areas are fully accessible.

AWARD:

2012 Building Brooklyn Award

SPONSORS:

Dunn Development Corp.

Cypress Hills Local Development Corporation

COMPLETED:

2012

WEINBERG GARDEN SENIOR RESIDENCE

2552 WEBB AVENUE, BRONX, NEW YORK

SENIOR HOUSING

This six-story, 72-unit project, rent-subsidized for low-income seniors, was funded by the U.S. Department of Housing and Urban Development. Built on the site of a former parking lot, it features landscaped outdoor gardens and a complete range of supportive and healthcare services, including short-stay rehabilitation and therapies, skilled nursing, home healthcare, adult day care, and social services.

DEVELOPER:

Jewish Home and Hospital

COMPLETED:

2010

1825 ATLANTIC AVENUE

BROOKLYN, NEW YORK

AFFORDABLE HOUSING

1825 Atlantic Avenue is a green family rental housing building with a day-care center on part of the first floor. At seven stories and 155,500 square feet, the building houses 150 dwelling units and ancillary community spaces, with parking on site, a children's day-care center, and a landscaped recreation area.

The building achieved Energy Star status through New York State Energy Research and Development Authority's Multifamily Performance Program.

SPONSORS:

Dunn Development Corp.

Acorn Housing Company

CONTRACTOR:

HLS Builders

COMPLETED:

2009

STERLING GLEN OF ROSLYN

100 ROSLYN ROAD, ROSLYN, NEW YORK

COLLABORATION, LUXURY SENIOR HOUSING

This 250-unit senior housing development is situated in an elegant park-like setting along a harbor. Amenities include 100,000 square feet of underground parking, multiple dining rooms, a library, bar, lounge, media room, fitness center, billiards room, card room, and beauty salon.

Conveniently located on Long Island's prestigious North Shore, this luxury community offers its residents art classes, cardio-fitness classes, yoga, computer classes, guest speakers and presentations, lectures and discussions, planned leisure and social events, as well as outings and other recreational activities.

EXECUTIVE ARCHITECT:
SLCE Architects

DESIGN ARCHITECT:
Robert A.M. Stern Architects

INTERIOR DESIGNER:
Culpeper McAuliffe and Meaders

DEVELOPER:
Sterling Glen

COMPLETED:
2007

DEKALB AVENUE APARTMENTS

910 DEKALB AVENUE, BROOKLYN, NEW YORK

AFFORDABLE HOUSING

Located in Bedford-Stuyvesant, Brooklyn, DeKalb Avenue Apartments was developed with support from the New York State Division of Housing and Community Renewal under its Low Income Housing Credit and Housing Trust Fund programs. At five stories and 50,000 square feet, the building is comprised of 64 affordable housing units, ranging from studios to two-bedrooms. These units provide housing for working families and formerly homeless adults with psychiatric disabilities. This innovative integration of people with special needs into a mainstream setting, along with the high-quality design and construction, has made this a model project expected to be widely replicated. The building features a carefully considered façade, high-quality finishes, and energy-efficient construction methods. Building amenities include a community room, library and computer room, tenant storage, and on-site support services.

AWARD:
Award of Excellence and 2004 Project of the Year from the New York State Association of Affordable Housing

SPONSOR:
Community Access

DEVELOPER:
Dunn Development Corp.

COMPLETED:
2004

THE HALLMARK

455 NORTH END AVENUE, NEW YORK, NEW YORK

COLLABORATION, ASSISTED LIVING

The Hallmark, developed by Brookdale Living Communities, is a 14-story, 240,000-square-foot facility containing 20 assisted-living units and 198 congregate-care units for seniors. Amenities include a community dining room, living room, billiards room, café, library, bar, beauty salon, media room, swimming pool, fitness center, arts and crafts space, and health clinic.

Located in Battery Park City, The Hallmark has guest accommodations, an outdoor garden area, and banking and postal services on site.

EXECUTIVE ARCHITECT:
SLCE Architects
DESIGN ARCHITECT:
Lucien Lagrange Architects
DEVELOPER:
Brookdale Living Communities
COMPLETED:
2001

DO NOT ENTER

LOTT RESIDENCE

1261 FIFTH AVENUE, NEW YORK, NEW YORK

SENIOR HOUSING

Located along Fifth Avenue in East Harlem with uninterrupted views of Central Park, the Lott Residence is a long-term care and assisted-living facility for seniors. At 14 stories and 98,000 square feet, the building is comprised of 124 studio apartments ranging from 400 to 450 square feet.

The building was designed with an abundance of public space to encourage socialization, provide a stimulating environment, and foster the perception that the entire building is part of each resident's home. The carpets, colors, finishes, and design of the public spaces are carefully planned to attract use on a daily basis. Among the many programmatic amenities, residents have access to music rooms, a library, exercise facilities, a game room, an arts and crafts room, lounges, and an outdoor garden. The building is operated under the New York State Department of Health's Assisted Living Program.

Clad in brick and granite, the building was constructed using poured-in-place flat-plate concrete placed on 100-foot-deep woodpiles. Precast concrete ornamentation is located at the third floor and at the top-floor level to accentuate the base and the top of the building.

DEVELOPER:

SFDS Development Corp.

COMPLETED:

2000

GEFFNER HOUSE, FORMERLY HOLLAND HOUSE

351 WEST 42ND STREET, NEW YORK, NEW YORK

SUPPORTIVE HOUSING

Geffner House is a 307-unit supportive single-room occupancy (SRO) building that provides permanent housing for low-income men and women, including people with serious and persistent mental illness; individuals who are recovering from drug or alcohol addiction; and people who are living with HIV/AIDS. This 1929 Art Deco, 21-story structure diagonally across from the Port Authority bus terminal was originally a single-room occupancy residential hotel, which eventually became an NYC property housing the homeless. Project Renewal took over management of the building, oversaw a series of major infrastructure upgrades, and initiated critical substance management and training programs for its resident population. The building was renamed Geffner House in honor of Project Renewal's founder, Ed Geffner. SLCE's commitment to providing architectural services to this and other important nonprofit organizations has long been an important component of its philosophy of providing shelter for all cogments of society

DEVELOPER:
Project Renewal

COMPLETED:
1995

CLINTON RESIDENCES

448 WEST 48TH STREET, NEW YORK, NEW YORK

SUPPORTIVE HOUSING

Project Renewal's Clinton Residence is a transitional treatment facility licensed and regulated by the NYS Office of Mental Health. The facility provides housing for 57 formerly homeless, single adults with chronic mental illness, some of whom have been dually diagnosed with a substance abuse disorder. This modestly scaled, neighborhood building, designed by SLCE, was the first ground-up project undertaken by Project Renewal, originally branded a Residential Care Center for Adults. Project Renewal has employed this formula of building new residences incrementally in well-established neighborhoods with great success over the decades, and now manages many thousands of apartment units throughout New York City for the previously homeless population.

DEVELOPER:

Project Renewal

COMPLETED:

1993

THE HIGH NOTE

BROWNSVILLE, BROOKLYN, NEW YORK

AFFORDABLE HOUSING

A 57,000-square-foot empty lot in the Brownsville neighborhood of Brooklyn will be transformed into an affordable housing and communal hub, with culturally infused programming to foster and incubate local self-expression. It will enliven the neighborhood by building an urban fabric and evolving streetscape that encourages community engagement with different institutions and with itself.

Conceived in two stages of nine-story buildings on Rockaway Avenue and Chester Street, the project will provide environmentally friendly energy sources through photovoltaic panels installed on the roofs. The public plaza and green space on the site—dubbed Art360—will facilitate performance art, congregation, and cultural activity.

DEVELOPER:
Dunn Development Corp.
COMPETITION SUBMISSION:
2018

THE ELIZA

4790 BROADWAY, NEW YORK, NEW YORK

AFFORDABLE HOUSING/MIXED-USE

The Department of Housing Preservation and Development (HPD), the New York City Housing Development Corp., and the New York Public Library (NYPL) have announced their plan to build a 175-unit affordable community in the uptown Washington Heights/Inwood neighborhood of Manhattan. The Eliza (named after Eliza Hamilton) will include a universal pre-K facility that will be operated by the New York City Department of Education and a new public library to be owned and operated by NYPL.

Located close to Inwood Park and Fort Tryon Park, the 14-story building will be a mix of studios and one-, two-, and three-bedroom apartments. In addition to a new three-level library branch, the project's amenities will include a gym, tenant lounge, playroom, terrace, roof garden, bicycle storage, and a laundry room.

All units will be affordable to extremely low-, very low-, and low-income households, as well as to formerly homeless families. The apartments will be restricted to individuals earning between \$20,040 and \$40,080 annually and households of three earning between \$34,360 and \$51,540. More than 20 percent of the units will be set aside for families of three earning less than \$26,000.

LIBRARY DESIGN CONSULTANT:

Marble Fairbanks

DEVELOPER:

Broadway Houses

COMPETITION SUBMISSION:

2018

“WHEN THE GOVERNMENT SAID, ‘WE SHOULD CONDUCT A STUDY,’ I WOULD FIND A WAY TO END THE PROCESS RIGHT THERE. I’M A MAN OF ACTION. JUST DO IT.”

Al Efron

4

COMMERCIAL & HOTELS

moxy
HOTEL
MISSION COFFEE CO

MOXY HOTEL

143 FULTON STREET,
NEW YORK, NEW YORK

HOTEL

Located in New York's Financial District, the Moxy Hotel at 143 Fulton will be the second addition to the brand's growing New York portfolio. Moxy Hotel is Marriott International's design-driven hospitality brand, focused on the three-star-tier millennial customer market.

The hotel, designed by SLCE, is on a through-block site between Ann Street and Fulton, with the hotel lobby opening on Ann Street and two levels of retail facing Fulton. At 30 stories and 129,000 square feet, the building is comprised of 298 hotel rooms, starting from the fifth floor. The first- and second-floor retail sits behind the double-elevation lobby, leading guests up to the sky lobby, with a central skylight. The third floor also contains a bar and multifunctional flex room for guests, creating an exciting communal space.

EXECUTIVE AND DESIGN ARCHITECT.
SLCE Architects

INTERIOR DESIGNER:
Stonehill & Taylor

DEVELOPER:
Tribeca Associates

EXPECTED COMPLETION:
2018

POD HOTEL

400 WEST 42ND STREET, NEW YORK, NEW YORK

MIXED-USE, HOTEL, RESIDENTIAL, RETAIL

POD Hotel is one of an increasing number of hotel/residential mixed-use projects that SLCE has designed in recent years. Buildings such as POD merge hospitality concepts with the usual complement of residential amenities. The exposed, roughly finished concrete structure contributes to the purposely edgy POD style sought by the brand, which identifies with the themes of this Times Square West and Hell's Kitchen neighborhood, many blocks removed from the bright lights associated with the heart of the Theater District. The POD Hotel comprises 257,722 square feet, rising 28 stories, and contains 665 hotel units and 40 residential units.

DEVELOPERS:

Friedman Group

Landis Group

COMPLETED:

2018

“WITH A PRICE TAG OF $75,000 A NIGHT, THE MARK HOTEL IS NOW OFFERING THE MOST EXPENSIVE HOTEL SUITE IN AMERICA.”

Cator Sparks, *Bloomberg*, September 28, 2018

The Mark Hotel is featured on pp. 322–323

T.J.maxx
Toys"R"us
KOHL'S
LEVEL 3
Century 21
TJ Maxx
LEVEL 2
Kohl's
Toys"R"us
Babies"R"us
LEVEL 1
GALLERIA
Pearle Vision
Payless
Mandee
JUNCTION BLVD
Red Mango
Sprint
Subway
5 Guys
Costco

REGO PARK CENTER

61-55 JUNCTION BOULEVARD, REGO PARK, NEW YORK

COLLABORATION, MIXED-USE, RETAIL/SHOPPING CENTER, RESIDENTIAL

SLCE worked as executive architect, in collaboration with Ehrenkrantz Eckstut & Kuhn Architects, to deliver Rego Park Center, an expansion of the existing Rego Park Mall just across the street at 62nd Drive. It is a mixed-use shopping mall of 1,332,133 square feet, with 307,867 square feet of apartments, on top of Rego Park Center, which was completed in 2010. The residential tower, branded The Alexander, is 20 stories high with 314 units, and was completed in 2016.

EXECUTIVE ARCHITECT:
SLCE Architects

DESIGN ARCHITECT:
Ehrenkrantz Eckstut & Kuhn Architects

DEVELOPER:
Vornado Realty Trust

COMPLETED:
2010–2016

HYATT CENTRIC TIMES SQUARE

135 WEST 45TH STREET, NEW YORK, NEW YORK

HOTEL

Situated between the Sixth Avenue business district and the Broadway/Seventh Avenue theater district, Hyatt Centric Times Square's 54-story glass exterior, designed by SLCE Architects, added a flourish to the Theater District. At the time of completion, the hotel was Manhattan's largest Hyatt Hotel at 311,000 square feet, comprising 538 hotel rooms. The spacious hotel rooms and suites give guests a premium apartment feel during their stay, compared to the much smaller product being built in this immediate area. The hotel also has a 4,200-square-foot spa, as well as a restaurant, rooftop lounge, and outdoor terrace. SLCE has completed a growing number of hotels, including the POD brand and the luxury Park Hyatt brand, and has witnessed a merging of hospitality concepts with its increasingly sophisticated residential work to a high degree.

INTERIORS:

George Wong Design

SPaN

DEVELOPER:

Extell Development Company

COMPLETED:

2013

PUB
CONNOLLY'S
RESTAURANT

510 MADISON AVENUE

NEW YORK, NEW YORK

COLLABORATION, MIXED-USE, OFFICE BUILDING, RETAIL

510 Madison is a 30-story, 311,640-square-foot Class A office building, with a LEED Gold certification. This modernist tower, designed in collaboration with MdeAS Architects, has clean façade lines and flexible interior spaces. The building includes a health club for the use of office tenants, a restaurant, and retail space on Madison Avenue.

EXECUTIVE ARCHITECT:
SLCE Architects

DESIGN ARCHITECT:
MdeAS Architects

DEVELOPER:
Macklowe Properties

COMPLETED:
2010

75 WALL RESIDENCES, HYATT ANDAZ

75 WALL STREET, NEW YORK, NEW YORK

HOTEL, LUXURY CONDOMINIUM, CONVERSION

This project consists of the rehabilitation of the existing 675,000-square-foot former Barclays Bank into exclusive high-end condominium homes and a luxury hotel. The repurposing of this building continued the redefinition of the New York City Financial District into a mixed-use area, with residential and hospitality uses adding to the attraction of this historic neighborhood.

Above the 15th floor, 410,000 square feet is dedicated to 350 condominium units, and an exclusive rooftop amenity with lounges and a breathtaking view of New York Harbor and downtown Brooklyn. The podium level includes a 220,000-square-foot, 250-room hotel and amenity spaces with lounges, a conference center, spa, and restaurant. With an interior design scheme by Rockwell Group, the hotel opened with much fanfare as the first Hyatt Andaz brand hotel in New York City.

INTERIOR DESIGN:
Rockwell Group
DEVELOPER:
The Hakimian Organization
COMPLETED:
2009

BLOOMBERG TOWER

731 LEXINGTON AVENUE,
NEW YORK, NEW YORK

COLLABORATION, MIXED-USE, OFFICE BUILDING, RETAIL, LUXURY RESIDENTIAL

As lead architect for this prominent 1.3-million-square-foot mixed-use project completed in 2005, SLCE Architects demonstrated its superior technical and organizational talents. The project, designed in collaboration with Pelli Clarke Pelli, occupies the entire 84,350-square-foot site of the former Alexander's Department Store. The building has retail on the lower floors with access to the subway system, commercial office space on levels three to 28, and 101 luxury residential apartments on levels 30 to 52. Bloomberg Headquarters, located at the building's base, required the latest security and information technology systems provided by the numerous sub-consultants and designers.

AWARD:

2004 Award of Merit, The Concrete Industry Board of New York

EXECUTIVE ARCHITECT:

SLCE Architects

DESIGN ARCHITECT:

Pelli Clarke Pelli

DEVELOPER:

Vornado Realty Trust

COMPLETED:

2005

THE GERMAN MISSION TO THE UNITED NATIONS

871 UNITED NATIONS PLAZA,
NEW YORK, NEW YORK

OFFICE, COMMERCIAL

The German Mission to the United Nations is a 23-story office building covering 103,500 square feet. This slender tower, with a typical office floor of a mere 4,500 square feet, while too small for conventional offices, has proven ideal for this Mission's criteria for natural light and fresh air through operable windows for every office worker. The taut granite and glass rectangular building shape is accentuated by chevrons of stainless steel trim, culminating in finials at the building's crown. The German Mission requirements for quality and its particular needs were satisfied by numerous sub-consultants and interior designers.

DEVELOPER:

The Albanese Organization

COMPLETED:

1996

Federal Republic of Germany
212.319.7327
SAMEDAY SERVICE
REPAIRS
DRY CLEAN
WEDDING GOWNS

712 FIFTH AVENUE

NEW YORK, NEW YORK

COLLABORATION, MIXED-USE, OFFICE BUILDING, RETAIL

712 Fifth Avenue is a 52-story, 500,000-square-foot office tower with a high-end retail base, located on "Limestone Alley" on Fifth Avenue alongside landmarks such as Rockefeller Center. Designed in collaboration with Kohn Pedersen Fox and Beyer Blinder Belle, the tower is predominantly sheathed in a light textured Indiana limestone façade, and the stone massing of the mixed-use building extends from a five-story solid masonry base. Incorporating a new public atrium and retail arcade with the landmarked Rizzoli and Coty structures, 712 Fifth Avenue respects the scale of West 56th Street's historic preservation district. Serving as the project's executive architect, SLCE successfully coordinated the huge team of designers and technical consultants.

EXECUTIVE ARCHITECT:
SLCE Architects
DESIGN ARCHITECTS:
Kohn Pedersen Fox Associates
Beyer Blinder Belle
DEVELOPER:
Taubman
COMPLETED:
1994

TWO GRAND CENTRAL TOWER

140 EAST 45TH STREET, NEW YORK, NEW YORK

OFFICE BUILDING

Two Grand Central Tower is a 43-story office building comprising 504,200 square feet of floor area. The sweeping curves of alternating horizontal bands of glass and brick combine with modulating setbacks to create a composition of distinction for the occupants of this Midtown Manhattan office tower. The triple-height lobby is entered from twin plazas fronting both 44th and 45th Streets. SLCE has completed numerous commercial office buildings through the decades, and continues to garner commissions for this building type.

DEVELOPER:

Macklowe Properties

COMPLETED:

1987

TEACHERS INSURANCE & ANNUITY ASSOCIATION

730 THIRD AVENUE, NEW YORK, NEW YORK

OFFICE BUILDING

SLCE Architects designed the 20-story addition to the existing structure at 730 Third Avenue for the expanding Teachers Insurance and Annuity Association. The 160,000-square-foot addition was designed to match the existing building, with gray brick, aluminum mullions, and glass spandrels. The new lobby which fronts Third Avenue was designed with contrasting coral marble and travertine. The retail spaces along the ground floor were redesigned, with new storefront windows and signage.

DEVELOPER:

TIAA-CREF

COMPLETED:

1992

HANOI EXHIBITION CENTER & TRADE, CULTURE AND ENTERTAINMENT CENTER

HANOI, VIETNAM

MIXED-USE, MASTERPLANNING

SLCE was invited by the Vietnam Bureau of Development to provide its vision for a new city within the city of Hanoi. It will be a diverse place to live, a vibrant place to work, and an exciting place to visit. It will be a 24/7 destination that reflects a new and modern Vietnam. The masterplan combines places for work, commerce, shopping, leisure, and living within a unified neighborhood, which addresses the program requirements and guidelines.

SLCE has provided integrated places for work and trade with an entertainment venue on par with anything internationally, and a state-of-the-art National Culture Center.

5

PUBLIC & INSTITUTIONAL

THE NEW SCHOOL
THE NEW SCHOOL
CHASE

THE NEW SCHOOL UNIVERSITY CENTER

63 FIFTH AVENUE, NEW YORK, NEW YORK

MIXED-USE, COLLABORATION, EDUCATION FACILITY, DORMITORY

In collaboration with Skidmore, Owings & Merrill (SOM), the New School's University Center is a mixed-use educational facility, located at the intersection of 14th Street and Fifth Avenue. SLCE provided layouts and massing for 150,000 square feet of student accommodations on the top nine floors, totaling 600 beds.

Designed by SOM, the lower seven floors of campus and educational spaces contain 12 classrooms, 28 studios, seven science labs, a library, a cafeteria, faculty offices, student lounges, and an 800-seat auditorium from the ground to the seventh floor. The building achieved LEED Gold certification.

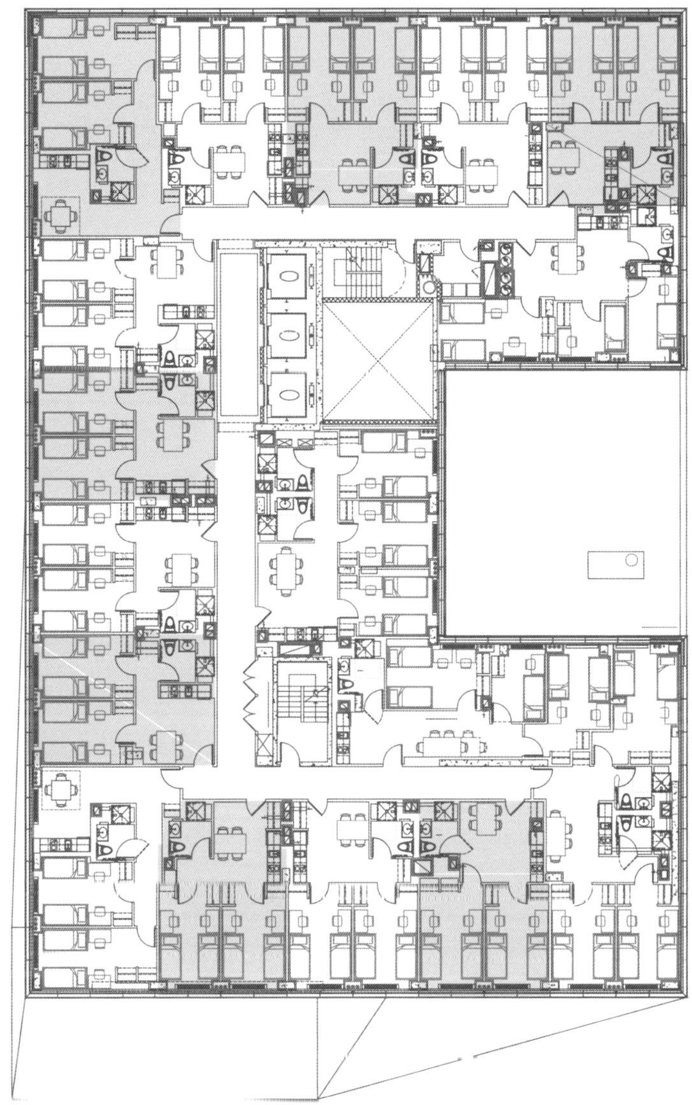

AWARD:

2015 American Institute of Architects (AIA) Committee on Architecture for Education (CAE): Education Facility Design Award of Excellence

RESIDENTIAL ARCHITECT:

SLCE Architects

DESIGN ARCHITECT:

Skidmore, Owings & Merrill

DEVELOPERS:

The Durst Organization

The New School

COMPLETED:

2013

CITY UNIVERSITY OF NEW YORK GRADUATE CENTER HOUSING

165 EAST 118TH STREET,
NEW YORK, NEW YORK
COLLABORATION, DORMITORY

In collaboration with Cooper, Robertson & Partners, CUNY's Hunter College Graduate Center Housing is comprised of eight stories and 65,000 square feet. The building houses 86 graduate students, post-doctoral fellows, and members of the faculty. The residence shares a plaza with CUNY's Hunter College School of Social Work campus, which was also designed by Cooper, Robertson & Partners.

SLCE's primary role for this project included the development of dormitory layouts, as well as construction documentation and administration of façade design. Building amenities include a student lounge, an exercise room, and a landscaped roof deck.

RESIDENTIAL ARCHITECT:
SLCE Architects
DESIGN ARCHITECT:
Cooper, Robertson & Partners
DEVELOPER:
Graduate Center Foundation Housing Corp.
COMPLETED:
2011

HEBREW INSTITUTE OF RIVERDALE

3700 HENRY HUDSON PARKWAY, BRONX, NEW YORK

SCHOOL

This project involved adding a new 35,000-square-foot school to an existing synagogue. The new building serves as the lobby for the now-renovated synagogue, and provides additional program areas such as offices, a social hall, Beit Midrash, rabbinical school, a new expansive lobby, and a variety of activity spaces.

OWNER:

Hebrew Institute of Riverdale

COMPLETED:

2010

HUNTER COLLEGE, SILBERMAN SCHOOL OF SOCIAL WORK

2180 THIRD AVENUE, NEW YORK, NEW YORK

COLLABORATION, EDUCATION

Located at Third Avenue from 118th Street to 119th Street, and stretching west toward Lexington Avenue, the Silberman School of Social Work was named after its two benefactors, Lois V. and Samuel J. Silberman. This education project spans 148,000 square feet and rises eight stories, comprising an auditorium, classrooms, lecture halls, laboratories, and offices. The entrance lobby was designed as an interior street, with the opportunity for school community gatherings and engagement with gallery space at street level. The building also houses the CUNY School of Public Health, the de Estudios Puertorriqueños Library, the Hunter Gallery, and the Brookdale Center.

EXECUTIVE ARCHITECT:

SLCE Architects

DESIGN ARCHITECT:

Cooper, Robertson & Partners

DEVELOPERS:

The Brodsky Organization

CUNY

COMPLETED:

2010

AHAVATH TORAH

240 BROAD STREET,
ENGLEWOOD, NEW JERSEY

SYNAGOGUE

This 63,287-square-foot Orthodox Jewish synagogue consists of four sanctuaries, a social hall, Beit Midrash, Mikvah, and an educational and office wing to serve the needs of roughly 1,500 congregants, with 70 parking spaces on site.

OWNER:

Ahavath Torah

COMPLETED:

2010

SOUTHTOWN ROOSEVELT ISLAND

405 MAIN STREET
NEW YORK, NEW YORK
COLLABORATION, DORMITORY

In collaboration with Gruzen Samton, Southtown Roosevelt Island features two buildings which were designed exclusively for the resident doctors and their families at Memorial Sloan-Kettering and Weill Cornell Medical College. The 16-story buildings feature over 360,000 square feet, providing 392 studios and one-, two-, and three-bedroom apartments. Amenity spaces include a community center and exercise facility in each respective building. In addition, a day-care center occupies the cellar of the Memorial Sloan-Kettering building. Gruzen Santom Architects was responsible for the exterior design, while SLCE was in charge of the interiors as well as apartment layouts, construction documents, and administration. The buildings were orientated to give all apartments views of Manhattan.

EXECUTIVE AND RESIDENTIAL ARCHITECT:
SLCE Architects
FAÇADE ARCHITECT:
Gruzen Samton Architects
DEVELOPERS:
Hudson Properties
Related Properties
COMPLETED:
2008

PRIMARY SCHOOL/ MIDDLE SCHOOL 194

2365 WATERBURY AVENUE, BRONX, NEW YORK

EDUCATION

SLCE designed this school with the New York City School Construction Authority as part of its successful Design Build Program. At four stories and 157,000 square feet, the 61 instructional spaces include kindergarten, pre-K, special education and dance classrooms, learning and science resource centers, and literacy and science labs. Other program spaces include an auditorium, cafeteria, gymnasium, and library and media center.

DEVELOPER:
DeMatteis Organization

COMPLETED:
2005

CHILDREN'S HOSPITAL AT MONTEFIORE MEDICAL CENTER

3415 BAINBRIDGE AVENUE, BRONX, NEW YORK

COLLABORATION, HEALTHCARE

In collaboration with MdeAS Architects and Rockwell Group, the Children's Hospital at Montefiore is a ten-story building comprised of a 109-bed pediatric center for infants, with age-specific floors for children and adolescents, and a pediatric critical care unit. Lower floors contain a day surgery center, ambulatory clinics, and a family learning center. An additional 10,000-square-foot renovation is dedicated to Pediatric Emergency, which serves 63,000 visits annually.

At ten stories, the building was designed with the in-patient sleeping units on the top three floors and out-patient facilities on the lower six floors. In order to provide efficient room layouts and a working room module, the top three floors were designed with a larger footprint than the floors below. The truss that is evident on the exterior provided the structural transfer needed to accommodate this at the seventh floor, which houses the mechanical equipment. The Rockwell Group envisioned the child-friendly design of the interior spaces, taking many cues from the Carl Sagan Discovery Center. The building was designed to convey information about the universe and science, making the experience for pediatric patients similar to that of a learning center rather than a hospital.

Designed as a hybrid wall system, the unitized building enclosure system prioritizes visual elements and creates a shadow-box effect. The superstructure was designed using a steel and metal decking along with column spacing specific to the in-patient room module.

EXECUTIVE ARCHITECT:
SLCE Architects
DESIGN ARCHITECTS:
MdeAS Architects
Rockwell Group
DEVELOPER:
Montefiore Medical Center
COMPLETED:
2001

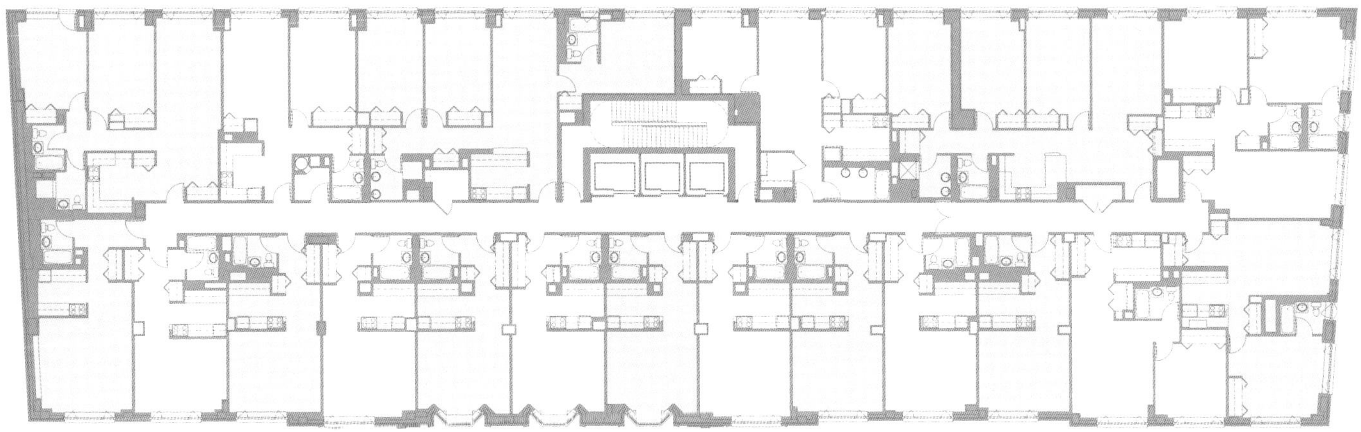

FEIL HALL, BROOKLYN LAW SCHOOL

205 STATE STREET, BROOKLYN, NEW YORK

COLLABORATION, DORMITORY

In collaboration with Robert A.M. Stern Architects, Feil Hall is a 22-story, 294,000-square-foot residential development for Brooklyn Law School. Catering to the needs of law students, the building's 239 units are laid out as small apartments, with communal amenities on the ground and top floors. At the time of completion, the building was a major part of the law school's ongoing effort to create a campus in the Borough Hall area of Brooklyn, and has allowed the school to attract an international graduate student population. Building amenities include a grand reception and lecture hall on the 22nd floor, along with two outdoor terraces with spectacular views of the New York City skyline and harbor. Additional amenities include Geraldo's Cafe, a 2,200-square-foot student café on the first floor, two levels of below-grade parking, dedicated on-site bicycle storage, and a student laundry facility.

EXECUTIVE ARCHITECT:
SLCE Architects
DESIGN ARCHITECT:
Robert A.M. Stern Architects
DEVELOPER:
Brooklyn Law School
COMPLETED:
2003

CARDOZO SCHOOL OF LAW AT YESHIVA UNIVERSITY

55 FIFTH AVENUE, NEW YORK, NEW YORK

RENOVATION, EDUCATION

This 14,000-square-foot modernization project involved the renovation of the main level of the Cardozo School of Law's library. The space provides essential library services such as a circulation desk, a reference desk, computer workstations, reading rooms, publications, and video playback.

DEVELOPER:

Yeshiva University

COMPLETED:

2003

“IN 2018, SLCE ARCHITECTS WERE RANKED THE MOST ACTIVE ARCHITECTURAL PRACTICE IN NEW YORK CITY, COMPLETING 87 PROJECTS ACROSS 20.69 MILLION SQUARE FEET.”

Ella Thorns, “Which Architecture Firms Are Building the Most in New York City?” *ArchDaily*, March 25, 2018

MARLENE MEYERSON JCC

334 AMSTERDAM AVENUE, NEW YORK, NEW YORK

COLLABORATION, COMMUNITY CENTER

Designed in collaboration with A.J. Diamond, Donald Schmitt and Company, the Marlene Meyerson JCC (formerly the JCC Westside Community Center) is located in the heart of the Upper West Side of Manhattan. A cornerstone of progressive programming in Manhattan, the JCC serves over 55,000 people annually and hosts over 1,200 programs each season, from after-school activities to fitness to volunteer programs.

The large and varied program is contained in a compact 14-story, 120,000-square-foot building. The small urban site caters to a vertically organized program, quite unusual for a community center. Three below-grade levels feature the auditorium, classrooms, and multimedia facilities. Programs stacked vertically above the ground-level lobby include an art gallery, a nursery school, café, fitness center, library, meditation space, gymnasium, swimming pool, and administrative offices. This stacking method was a challenge in terms of structure and technicalities. Since a number of the programs require column-free space, entire levels had to be structurally and mechanically reimagined to accommodate the demand.

EXECUTIVE ARCHITECT:

SLCE Architects

DESIGN ARCHITECT:

A.J. Diamond, Donald Schmitt and Company

DEVELOPER:

Jewish Community Center

COMPLETED:

2001

PARK
OPEN 24 HOURS
GARAGE

FORDHAM UNIVERSITY RESIDENCE HALL, LINCOLN CENTER

NEW YORK, NEW YORK

EDUCATION, RESIDENCE HALL

Fordham University Residence Hall on West 60th Street at Lincoln Center is a 20-story, reinforced concrete frame structure providing accommodation for 877 students in 286,500 square feet of space. Typical two- and three-bedroom suites consist of kitchens, living/dining rooms, and bathrooms. The richly detailed exterior of the building is composed of generously proportioned windows set in façades made up of two brick colors and accents of cast stone. The building's color palette conforms to Lincoln Center's travertine and limestone composition.

OWNER:

Fordham University

COMPLETED:

2000

BLOOMFIELD HEALTHCARE CENTER

355 PARK AVENUE, BLOOMFIELD, CONNECTICUT

NURSING FACILITY, RENOVATION, EXPANSION

Bloomfield Healthcare Center is a nursing and rehabilitation center in Bloomfield, Connecticut. SLCE designed the renovation and expansion of the existing one-story, 120-bed, skilled nursing facility of 55,000 square feet.

The main objective was to eliminate the existing four-bedded rooms and join the four existing wings, now connected by two additional links, each housing nine beds and one new centrally located nurses' station. The existing kitchen, dining room, and physical therapy units were upgraded and expanded with smaller additions, and a new porte-cochère was added.

OWNER:
National Healthcare Associates

COMPLETED:
2000

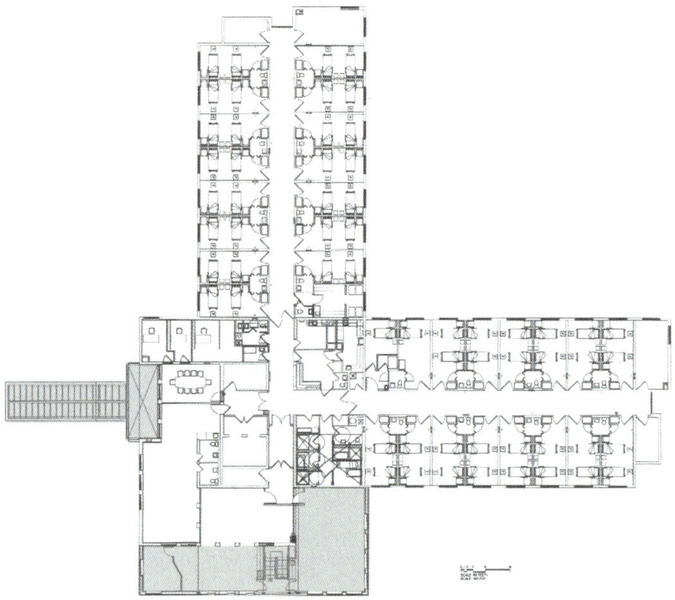

MAPLE VIEW MANOR

856 MAPLE STREET, ROCKY HILL, CONNECTICUT

NURSING FACILITY

The scope of this project was to renovate and expand an existing two-story skilled nursing facility comprising 35,000 square feet. A new two-story addition was built in order to expand existing dining, physical therapy, occupational therapy, and nursing departments. The nurses' station and bathing suites were upgraded to meet current code. Resident rooms were upgraded with new plumbing fixtures, HVAC, and finishes. A new two-story glass-enclosed lobby was added with a new porte-cochère.

OWNER:

National Healthcare Associates

COMPLETED:

2000

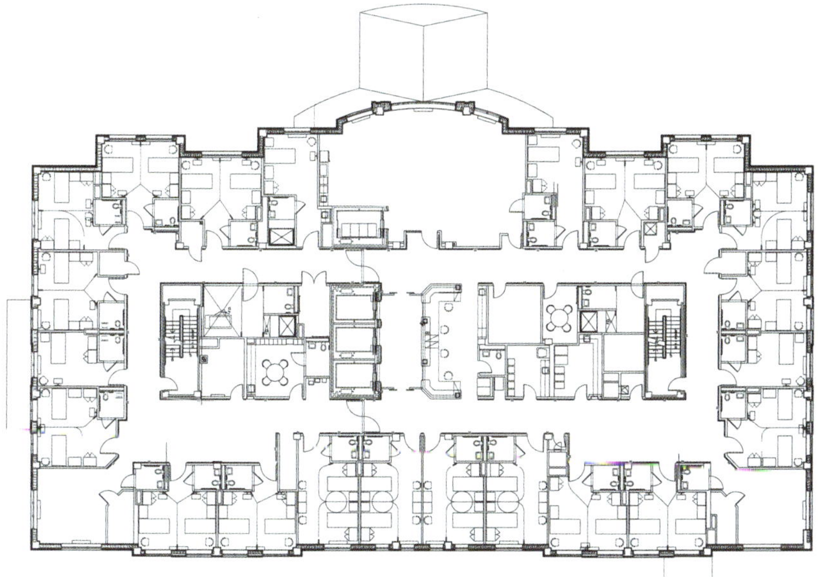

HAYM SALOMON HOME

2340 CROPSEY AVENUE,
BROOKLYN, NEW YORK

SKILLED NURSING FACILITY

Haym Salomon Home is a 240-bed, 135,000-square-foot skilled nursing facility with adult day care and full physical and occupational therapy programs, as well as dental and medical clinics.

OWNER:
Haym Salomon Home

COMPLETED:
1998

HUNTINGTON HILLS

EAST NORTH PORT RESIDENTIAL HEALTH,
LONG ISLAND EXPRESSWAY
AND ROUTE 110, NEW YORK

HEALTHCARE

This 187,000-square-foot facility provides 320 skilled nursing bed units, including Alzheimer's and ventilator-dependent wings on two floors, plus a partial basement. Strict zoning, setback and height constraints, and the need to maintain the residential character of the adjoining neighborhood dictated careful siting within the topographical contours.

DEVELOPER:
National Health Care Associates

COMPLETED:
1998

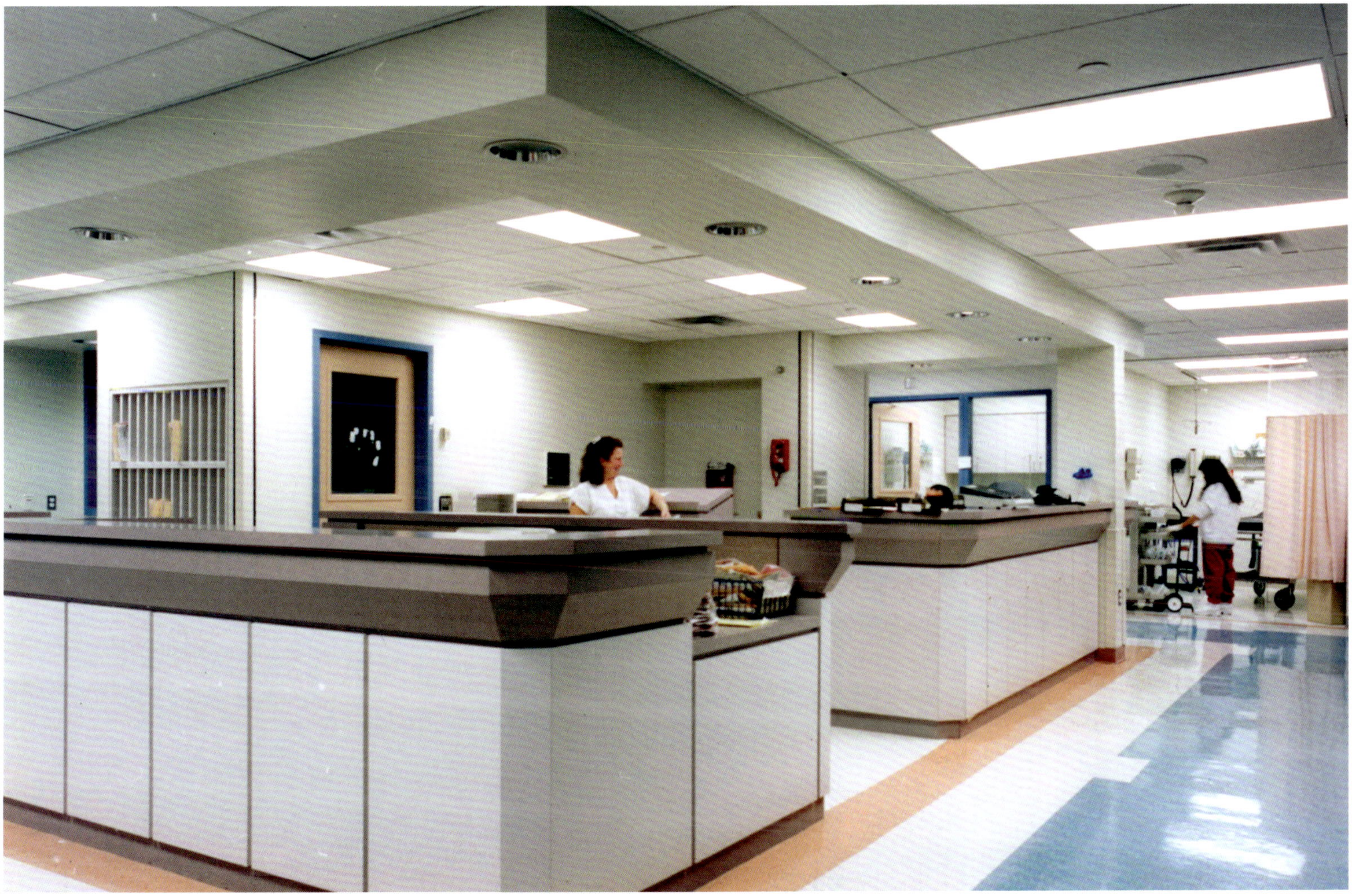

BROOKDALE UNIVERSITY & MEDICAL CENTER, ADULT EMERGENCY DEPARTMENT

1 BROOKDALE PLAZA, BROOKLYN, NEW YORK

MEDICAL CENTER

This $2.7-million reconstruction consists of an adult treatment area with separate support spaces, a pediatric treatment area, radiology imaging suite, radiographic rooms, CT scanner, and separate holding and reading areas.

DEVELOPER:
Brookdale University Hospital & Medical Center

COMPLETED:
1997

PORT RICHMOND HIGH SCHOOL

ST. JOSEPHS AVENUE/45 INNIS STREET, STATEN ISLAND, NEW YORK

EDUCATION

The scope of this project included both the modernization of and a new addition to Port Richmond High School in Staten Island. Modernization of the three-story-plus basement, 164,000-square-foot original school provided a uniform transition into the new three-story, 64,500-square-foot addition. In order to accommodate 2,500 students and 320 staff members, the new addition is comprised of 20 classrooms, administrative and counseling offices, seven state-of-the-art laboratories, studios and a shop, and a double-height entry lobby. The building's detailed exterior combines flamed granite, brick, and limestone-colored precast concrete with iron fencing to complement the richness of the adjoining Georgian buildings. The new addition provided the school with a new entrance portico and entrance lobby. Additionally, a new corridor linked the old school to the new addition, allowing circulation on all floors.

DEVELOPERS:

New York City Board of Education

New York City School Construction Authority

COMPLETED:

1996

KINGSBROOK JEWISH MEDICAL CENTER

585 SCHENECTADY AVENUE, BROOKLYN, NEW YORK

MEDICAL CENTER

As the primary Kingsbrook Jewish Medical Center architect for nearly three decades, SLCE has completed numerous new facilities as well as major modernization projects. The Briger Pavilion, for example, was completed in 1990. This 140-bed acute-care wing with a ten-bed intensive care unit and a ten-bed coronary care unit is an example of how new structures can integrate both aesthetically and functionally into an existing campus. Other SLCE projects at Kingsbrook have included the Rutland Nursing Home, the Geriatric Psychiatric Unit, the Traumatic Brain Injury & Coma Recovery Unit, and the David Minkin Rehabilitation Institute.

DEVELOPER:
Kingsbrook Medical Center

COMPLETED:
1990

HELMSLEY MEDICAL TOWER

1320 YORK AVENUE, NEW YORK, NEW YORK

HEALTHCARE

Designed by SLCE and completed in 1987, Helmsley Medical Tower's 36 stories contain medical offices in its base and nurses' and physicians' residences in the tower. It remains the tallest structure within the Cornell Medical Center campus complex, all of which was designed in the Avignon gothic style. The tower has a commanding presence on York Avenue and East 70th street, its alternating vertical shafts of brick piers and glass and aluminum curtain walls accentuating its verticality, crowned with the obligatory gothic arches and pediments for which this campus is known. SLCE has been involved in additional buildings over the years on both this and other medical campuses in New York City, including Beth Israel Mt. Sinai and Kingsbrook medical centers.

DEVELOPER:

Cornell Medical Center

COMPLETED:

1987

“THE MOST SUCCESSFUL JOB IS A HANDSOME BUILDING THAT RENTS OR SELLS QUICKLY—AND IS WITHIN THE COST RESTRAINTS ESTABLISHED BY THE DEVELOPER.”

Peter Claman

BETH ISRAEL MEDICAL CENTER

FIRST AVENUE AT 16TH STREET,
NEW YORK, NEW YORK

HOSPITAL, EXPANSION, MODERNIZATION

Founded in 1889, Beth Israel Medical Center is a 799-bed teaching hospital on Manhattan's Lower East Side. During the 1960s, SLCE was responsible for the modernization and expansion of several buildings for the hospital. These included Baird Hall, a 17-story staff residence building (completed in 1963); Fireman Hall, a nursing school and nurses' dormitory, and Linsky Pavilion, an acute-care facility with 180 semi-private bedrooms, a surgical department, radiographic department, and radiology department (both completed in 1966); and Gillman Hall, a 24-story building of staff residences (completed in 1969).

DEVELOPER:
Beth Israel Medical Center

COMPLETED:
1963–1969

6

RENOVATION & REHABILITATION

THE WOOLWORTH BUILDING

2 PARK PLACE, NEW YORK, NEW YORK

COLLABORATION, ADAPTIVE REUSE, LUXURY CONDOMINIUM

Perfectly illustrating SLCE's active role in the conversions of marginal office space to premier condominium residences, the Woolworth Building might just be the jewel in the crown. The Woolworth Building soars above City Hall Park at the gateway to Tribeca. Originally designed by Cass Gilbert in 1913, the building was designed as a neo-gothic skyscraper and dubbed "The Cathedral of Commerce." Unprecedented in size and sophistication, the Woolworth stood as the tallest building in the world until 1930. It included the fastest and highest elevators of its day and was promised by F.W. Woolworth to "long herald the march of progress down through the corridors of time." Today, this stately tower retains its elegance on the skyline of Lower Manhattan.

In collaboration with The Office of Thierry Despont, SLCE worked closely with the Landmarks Preservation Commission and Higgins Quasebarth & Partners to assure the integrity of the

building's architectural exterior during its conversion and restoration. The scope of the conversion includes the upper 26 floors, which are being masterfully transformed to include 33 luxury units spanning 159,000 square feet. The building's six-story pinnacle will be converted into a truly unique penthouse. This space required immense structural modification and creative solutions to façade and envelope conditions.

New egress stairs were added in addition to new high-speed elevators, which give residents quick access to their apartments that start at the 29th floor and basement amenity levels. Modifications were made to make way for modern mechanical, electrical, and plumbing systems, which independently service the new residential floors. These modifications were made in an effort to infuse 21st-century luxuries into the building's underutilized, premium, and historic space.

EXECUTIVE ARCHITECT:
SLCE Architects

INTERIOR DESIGNER:
The Office of Thierry Despont

DEVELOPER:
Alchemy

EXPECTED COMPLETION:
2019

RANDOLPH HOUSES

214–243 WEST 114TH STREET, NEW YORK, NEW YORK

REHABILITATION

AWARDS:

Excellence in Historic Preservation Awards by the Preservation League of New York State

Lucy G. Moses Preservation Award from the New York Landmarks Conservancy

2018 New York State Historic Preservation Award from the Office of Parks, Recreation and Historic Preservation

DEVELOPER:

Trinity Financial

COMPLETED:

Phase I: 2016

Phase II: 2018

Much like their surrounding West Harlem neighborhood, the Randolph Houses have a rich history. Multiple owners and varying levels of neglect had left an entire block of late 19th-century tenement buildings largely vacant. The limestone, brick, and brownstone façades had been stripped of ornament, patched haphazardly, and painted, while the interiors deteriorated. By the early 2000s, many of the buildings were emptied and slated for demolition, but following their listing on the National Register of Historic Places, New York City issued a Request for Proposals for redevelopment of the buildings as affordable and public housing.

The West 114th Street historic district, as listed on the National Register of Historic Places, is comprised of 37 buildings (the 36 residential buildings of Randolph Houses and one school). The five-story residential buildings in the district are classified as Old Law Tenement buildings, built in seven phases from 1895 to 1899, and designed by Neville & Bagge and John P. Leo and Kerby & Co. Old Law Tenements are quite difficult to redesign due to constraints on light and air imposed by the lot sizing and coverage.

The redesign strategy was to merge the individual lots into two larger zoning lots and create three contiguous buildings from the 36 independent ones. Eleven buildings were combined to create Building A, while another eleven were combined to create Building B. The remaining buildings would become Building C during phase II of the project. Each new building was internally connected with a five-foot-wide interior corridor. To provide common, accessible entry to each building, the ground floor was lowered and elevators were added at central lobbies. The historic façade of each building was meticulously cleaned and repaired, and new cast-iron window surrounds, windows, and doors were installed. Existing cornices were repaired, and new sheet-metal replicas were installed where originals had long been missing. The interior spaces were gut-renovated and converted into 168 units of affordable and public housing, in addition to 3,000 square feet of community space including a library, computer rooms, communal spaces, and an outdoor terrace.

The project, which combined state and federal historic preservation tax credits with low-income housing tax credits and other city financing, serves as a model for the preservation and adaptive reuse of historic buildings for affordable housing and for creative solutions for improving public housing. The rehabilitation of the Randolph Houses maintains the 19th-century New York streetscape while introducing standards of modern living. Phase I of the project was completed in 2016; phase II was completed in 2018 for a total of 355,000 square feet.

108 LEONARD

NEW YORK, NEW YORK

RENOVATION, CONDOMINIUM

Originally designed by McKim, Mead & White as the home of the New York Life Insurance Company, 108 Leonard was constructed in two phases, during the years 1894–1904. It is a designated New York City Landmark, and is listed on the National Register of Historic Places. The landmark designation includes the Italian Renaissance Revival-style exterior, and several interior spaces, including the main entry lobby, grand banking hall, several interior staircases, and beautifully constructed interior office spaces.

SLCE worked closely with Elad Group, who managed the development of the project, and design firm Jeffrey Beers International to assure the integrity of the building's architecture during its conversion and restoration. The conversion includes 167 masterfully designed residential condominium units across the building's 420,000 square feet. Amenity spaces and a private motor reception were created at the lower levels. Three vertical elevator and stair cores were created to allow the most flexible residential planning, and the upper level and roof were reconstructed using modern materials to allow full access to rooftop gardens and private exterior terraces.

Several historical interior landmarks required removal, preservation, and relocating within the conversion, and SLCE worked closely with consultants and the Landmarks Preservation Commission to ensure success in this unique endeavor.

EXECUTIVE ARCHITECT:
SLCE Architects

INTERIOR DESIGNER:
Jeffrey Beers International

DEVELOPER:
The Elad Group

EXPECTED COMPLETION:
2019

ONE WALL STREET

NEW YORK, NEW YORK

CONVERSION, MIXED-USE, LUXURY CONDOMINIUM, RETAIL

One Wall Street is an Art Deco office building In New York City. The North Tower, designed by Ralph Walker, was built in 1931 and is a landmarked building. The South Tower addition was built in 1963. Macklowe Properties purchased the 51-story property in 2014, and is in the process of converting it into 566 high-end luxury condominiums, and retail spaces at the lower levels. Residents will enjoy amenities such as a golf simulator, gym, indoor and outdoor lounge, and 75-foot by 20-foot swimming pool, among other items including numerous private terraces. Floor area was reallocated to allow for additional apartments and amenity spaces above the South Tower, maximizing the value of the property.

EXECUTIVE ARCHITECT:

SLCE Architects

INTERIORS:

Robert A.M. Stern Architects

DEVELOPER:

Macklowe Properties

EXPECTED COMPLETION:

2020

HOWARD BEACH SENIOR HOUSING

155-55 CROSS BAY BOULEVARD,
HOWARD BEACH, NEW YORK
REHABILITATION, SENIOR HOUSING

Howard Beach was an existing four-story hospital that was converted into low-income senior housing. At 115,000 square feet, the building is comprised of 84 units ranging from studios to one-bedroom apartments for low-income seniors, and 12 units on the first floor which are occupied by people with developmental disabilities. A senior center is located on the first floor along with activity rooms, supportive offices, and laundry room. Most levels feature a centrally located lounge for residents.

DEVELOPER:
Catholic Charities of Brooklyn and Queens
COMPLETED:
2013

THE LEONARD

350 BROADWAY, NEW YORK, NEW YORK

CONVERSION, MIXED-USE, LUXURY CONDOMINIUM, RETAIL

This is a conversion of a 139,000-square-foot, 12-story prewar building previously occupied by office space. The building was rehabilitated to include 66 one-, two-, and three-bedroom high-end luxury condominiums, lofts, and penthouses. In addition, a fitness center, a children's playroom, and a roof terrace were added as common amenities. The first floor facing Broadway includes a small retail space.

Extensive restoration of the façade and upgrades to meet recent building codes along with luxurious finishes are part of the project.

DEVELOPER:
Bizzi & Partners

COMPLETED:
2013

1212 FIFTH AVENUE

NEW YORK, NEW YORK

CONVERSION, LUXURY CONDOMINIUM

This project consisted of the adaptive reuse of a 113,000-square-foot apartment building on Central Park into 58 luxury condominiums.

The complete approach was one of extreme sensitivity to the prewar elegance of the original building. This included coordination of all new interiors with the restoration of existing plaster coffered ceilings and moldings; a complete façade restoration; new windows throughout; new HVAC, plumbing, and electricity; and a full lobby renovation and restoration.

Occupying its place on Central Park since the 1920s, 1212 Fifth Avenue exemplifies the craftsmanship and attention to detail that distinguishes prewar architecture. The building was designed in 1925 by George and Edward Blum, brothers who trained at the École des Beaux-Arts in Paris.

DEVELOPERS:

Fetner Properties

The Durst Organization

COMPLETED:

2011

TWELVE TWELVE
FIFTH AVENUE

184 KENT AVENUE

BROOKLYN, NEW YORK

ADAPTIVE REUSE, MARKET-RATE RENTAL

This adaptive reuse project involved the conversion and restoration of a Cass Gilbert-designed warehouse into beautiful contemporary apartments. In addition to being situated near many shops and restaurants in the thriving Williamsburg and Greenpoint neighborhoods, the building offers striking views of Manhattan from its site along the East River. The building has six stories and is comprised of 360 units.

DEVELOPER:
J.M.H Development

COMPLETED:
2010

APPLE BANK

2112 BROADWAY, NEW YORK, NEW YORK

ADAPTIVE REUSE, CONDOMINIUM

Located in the heart of the Upper West Side and adjacent to the Upper West Side historic district, Apple Bank, itself a listed building, was designed in 1928 as a Federal Reserve Bank in miniature, with a theatrically high banking hall and extensive cellar vault rooms. Only the upper floors were converted to a small number of larger for-sale apartments, with ground-floor bank uses maintained. A complete restoration of the façade and bank hall was also undertaken. SLCE Architects has enjoyed an increasing share of repurposed landmarked buildings, which lend a huge contribution to the character of the neighborhoods in which they reside.

DEVELOPER:

Stahl Real Estate

COMPLETED:

2008

Apple
Bank
201

THE MARK HOTEL

25 EAST 77TH STREET, NEW YORK, NEW YORK

ADAPTIVE REUSE, MIXED-USE, HOTEL, LUXURY CONDOMINIUM

The Mark Hotel, built in 1927 and designed by architects Schwartz & Gross, fronts Madison Avenue on New York's iconic Upper East Side.

At 15 stories, this luxury condo-hotel conversion is comprised of 118 hotel rooms and 42 apartments. The interiors of the hotel and apartments were designed by award-winning French designer Jacques Grange. Residents of The Mark can enjoy 24-hour concierge service, valet service, a fitness center, and a rooftop deck. The hotel is also home to The Frédéric Fekkai Salon and the highly acclaimed Mark Restaurant and The Mark Bar.

SLCE has played a growing role in repurposing landmarked properties for improved viability and changing markets. The Mark Hotel is an example of such a building, ideally suited to conversion into luxury condos while maintaining hotel functions on the lower floors.

AWARD:

Merit for Interior Design/Tenant Improvement, Engineering News-Records New York Constructions' Best of 2009

INTERIOR DESIGNER:

Jacques Grange

DEVELOPER:

HFZ Capital

COMPLETED:

2008

88 GREENWICH STREET

NEW YORK, NEW YORK

CONVERSION, MARKET-RATE RENTAL

In line with the trend of office to residential conversion projects in Lower Manhattan, 88 Greenwich Street aimed to preserve the building's historic 1929 Art Deco façade, while transforming the interior into 457 market-rate rental apartments. The units feature ten-foot ceilings and oversized windows to take advantage of the sweeping views of Lower Manhattan and the harbor. In addition to the residential units, amenity spaces include a fitness center, roof terrace, business center, and game room.

DEVELOPER:
Worldwide Holdings

COMPLETED:
2006

CIPRIANI CLUB RESIDENCES AT 55 WALL STREET

NEW YORK, NEW YORK

CONVERSION, MIXED-USE, LUXURY CONDOMINIUM, RESTAURANT, RETAIL

The Cipriani Club Residences include the adaptive reuse of 106,000 square feet into 106 fully furnished luxury condominiums, new penthouse duplex additions, and a private rooftop amenity space, all atop the 12,000-square-foot 60-foot-high Exchange Floor Ballroom.

The conversion of this historic building was at the forefront of redefining the New York City Financial District into a mixed-use area, with residential use adding to the activity of this historic neighborhood.

With an interior design by Tsao & McKown, the 26,000-square-foot Cipriani Club 55 includes a restaurant and bar, private library, traditional barber shop, business lounge, full-service spa, billiards room, screening room, and a boutique. 55 Wall Street was built in 1842 as the Merchant Exchange, became home to the New York Stock Exchange until 1854, and later housed the U.S. Custom House. The building became a New York City Landmark in 1965; one of the first buildings to be designated. It is also listed on the National Register of Historic Places.

DEVELOPERS:
Cipriani
The Witkoff Group

COMPLETED:
2007

THE OCTAGON, ROOSEVELT ISLAND

888 MAIN STREET, NEW YORK, NEW YORK

CONVERSION, AFFORDABLE HOUSING

Octagon Park Apartments is a newly constructed 80/20 multi-family development, designed in collaboration with Becker and Becker, and built around the Landmark Octagon building. At 13 stories and 425,000 square feet, this rental building is comprised of 500 apartments, of which 20 percent are affordable. The Landmark Octagon building has been renovated to house the development lobby and resident amenities. Landscaped exterior spaces with tennis courts, swimming pool, and parking are also provided. The building is designed with precast concrete exterior panels and window wall. Solar panels provide energy for the majority of the public space.

DEVELOPER:
Octagon L.P. Bruce Becker

COMPLETED:
2006

ST. LUCY AND ST. PATRICK'S FAMILY HOUSING

171 TAAFFE PLACE, BROOKLYN, NEW YORK

CONVERSION, AFFORDABLE HOUSING

St. Lucy and St. Patrick's was an existing parochial school located in Brooklyn, which underwent alteration and rehabilitation to become low-income housing under the New York State Department of Housing and Community Renewal Program. The three-story plus basement, 62,000-square-foot building houses 47 apartment units along with community spaces for residents. Within the double-height existing school gymnasium, an intermediate floor was created to increase the number of units within the development.

AWARD:

Queens County Builders and Contractors Excellence in Design Award

DEVELOPER:

Catholic Charities of Brooklyn and Queens

COMPLETED:

2000

WESTBURY HOTEL

15 EAST 69TH STREET, NEW YORK, NEW YORK

ADAPTIVE REUSE, CONVERSION,
LUXURY CONDOMINIUMS

The storied, prewar Westbury Hotel became ripe for conversion to luxury residential condominiums as the result of a burgeoning residential market in this rarified East Side, landmarked neighborhood close to Central Park. The 47 luxury residential apartment units sold briskly due to the appeal of modern conveniences coupled with prewar detailing. SLCE worked closely with the Landmarks Preservation Commission and the developer on this successful conversion. The entire masonry exterior was restored to its prewar elegance, and floor area was added to the upper floors, which actually enhanced the overall rooftop composition.

DEVELOPER:
Chelsfield

COMPLETED:
1999

71 BROADWAY

NEW YORK, NEW YORK

CONVERSION, LUXURY RENTAL

Located opposite Trinity Church and the foot of Wall Street, 71 Broadway is a 21-story office building designed in the Classical Revival style and completed in 1898. Vacated by the U.S. Steel Corporation in 1976, 71 Broadway slowly fell into disrepair until a burgeoning residential market discovered a healthy appetite for downtown, high-ceilinged, and loft-like conversions. SLCE worked closely with the Landmarks Preservation Commission on the building's façade restoration and new storefront, and designed spacious rental apartments for this end of the market. SLCE has subsequently garnered numerous such commissions in downtown Manhattan, contributing to this newfound 24/7 neighborhood.

DEVELOPER:
World Wide Group

COMPLETED:
1998

71
COLORTEK
1 HOUR PHOTO
International
HAIRCUTTERS
Champs
SIGNATURE BANK
CLEANER

LUXURY RENTALS

LE RIVAGE

21 WEST STREET, NEW YORK, NEW YORK

CONVERSION, LUXURY RENTAL

Le Rivage represents a growing trend in major urban areas to convert architecturally significant properties from underperforming office uses to luxury housing with state-of-the-art features. SLCE Architects, through its insightful floor plans and focus on market-driven amenities, has become a major player in this field. High ceilings, home offices, and ample storage closets combined with restored prewar details have become an attractive alternative to new construction for discriminating buyers and renters.

DEVELOPER:

Rose Associates

COMPLETED:

1998

LANDMARK ON MAIN STREET

MAIN STREET SCHOOL, 232 MAIN STREET, PORT WASHINGTON, NEW YORK

REHABILITATION, AFFORDABLE HOUSING

Originally built in 1907, this 78,000-square-foot landmarked school in Port Washington has been converted into 60 affordable apartments for senior citizens. The project also includes a community center which includes a day-care center, parent resource center, Alzheimer's center, teen sports center with an indoor basketball court, a 500-seat theater, and a children's sports facility. Landmark on Main Street received a 1996 New York State Historic Preservation Award from the State Office of Parks, Recreation and Historic Preservation.

AWARD:

New York State Historic Preservation Award, 1996

DEVELOPER:

Landmark Housing Development Fund Corporation

COMPLETED:

1996

MERCY GARDENS

249 CLASSON AVENUE, BROOKLYN, NEW YORK

REHABILITATION, AFFORDABLE HOUSING

This turn-of-the-century, U-shaped, five-story plus basement convent building belonging to the Sisters of Mercy was partially converted to a single-room occupancy (SRO) building for formerly homeless women. 78 studio units along with a commercial kitchen, dining rooms, and activity spaces for residents are provided within the 36,000-square-foot area of the rehabilitation and conversion of the building, which was completed in July 1993.

In a second phase, the Sisters of Mercy upgraded and converted the remainder of the building for retired nuns from their order. Catholic Charities of Brooklyn and Queens purchased and operate the SRO part of the converted building. This second phase of the rehabilitation, for the retirement portion of the building, was completed in 1998.

DEVELOPER:

Catholic Charities of Brooklyn and Queens

COMPLETED:

1993

1255 FIFTH AVENUE

NEW YORK, NEW YORK

CONVERSION, LUXURY CONDOMINIUM

Originally a nursing home in 1925, and located just above 107th Street along the north stretch of Museum Mile fronting Central Park, 1255 Fifth Avenue was an early conversion to residential condominiums in the late 1980s as the residential market inexorably marched north of 96th Street. SLCE took special care to retain and restore the original façade detailing of this prewar gem. At eight stories, the entire structure comprises a mere 59 larger residences.

DEVELOPER:

Millennium Properties

COMPLETED:

1985

“THE RENOVATION [OF THE RANDOLPH HOUSES] TAKES A STAND ABOUT MAINTAINING HARLEM FABRIC IN THIS MOMENT OF HUGE CHANGE, AND ALSO MAINTAINING LOW-INCOME HOUSING… YOU’VE GOT TO ADMIRE THOSE ARCHITECTS. THEY’RE IN THE TRENCHES, TRYING TO DO SOMETHING IMPOSSIBLE.”

Richard Plunz, from Jonathan Lerner, “A Preservation Paradox,”
Oculus, Fall 2016
The Randolph Houses are featured on pp. 308–309

PORTFOLIO OF PROJECTS, 1941–2018

1 BOERUM PLACE
Brooklyn, New York
Market-Rate Residential Rental

2 LINCOLN SQUARE
60 West 66th Street
New York, New York
Market-Rate Residential Rental
Completed: 1974

4 ALBANY STREET
New York, New York
Adaptive Reuse, Conversion

4 WEST 21ST STREET
New York, New York
Luxury Residential Condominium
Completed: 2006

7 EAST 86TH STREET
New York, New York
Market-Rate Residential Rental
Completed: 1961

10 HANOVER SQUARE
New York, New York
Adaptive Reuse, Conversion, Market-Rate Rental
Completed: 2006–2009

11 AVENUE C
New York, New York
Market-Rate Residential Condominium

11 BARROW STREET
New York, New York
Adaptive Reuse

15 WILLIAM STREET
New York, New York
Market-Rate Residential Rental
Completed: 2008

21 EAST 12TH STREET (pictured p. 339)
New York, New York
Market-Rate Residential Condominium
Design Architect: Selldorf Architects

25 WEST 128TH STREET
New York, New York
Affordable Housing
Completed: 2009

29–37 41ST AVENUE
Long Island City, New York
Mixed-Use, Residential, Dormitory

36–20 STEINWAY STREET
Long Island City, New York
Market-Rate Residential Rental

38–46 WEST 33RD STREET
New York, New York
Mixed-Use, Residential, Retail

39 WHITEHALL STREET
New York, New York
Adaptive Reuse, Recycled

44 WEST 66TH STREET
New York, New York
Mixed-Use, Residential, Retail

47 CLINTON PLACE
New Rochelle, New York
Affordable Housing
Completed: 2009

50 NORTH FIFTH STREET
Brooklyn, New York
Market-Rate Residential Condominium
Completed: 2013

55 BANK STREET – PHASE 1
White Plains, New York
Market-Rate Residential Rental

61 JANE STREET (FRONTING HUDSON STREET)
New York, New York
Market-Rate Residential Condominium
Completed: 1963

69 WEST NINTH STREET
New York, New York
Market-Rate Residential Condominium
Completed: 1959

72ND AVENUE AND 110TH STREET
Forest Hills, New York
Residential
Completed: 1970s

21 East 12th Street

73 WOOSTER STREET

New York, New York

Adaptive Reuse, Conversion, Market-Rate Condominium

Completed: 2004

101 WEST 55TH STREET

New York, New York

Adaptive Reuse, Recycled, Market-Rate Rental

Completed: 1970s

111 BARROW STREET

New York, New York

Adaptive Reuse, Recycled

Completed: 1987

118 FULTON STREET

New York, New York

Market-Rate Residential Rental

118 MADISON AVENUE

New York, New York

Adaptive Reuse, Recycled, Market-Rate Rental

Completed: 1970s

120 FIFTH AVENUE

Brooklyn, New York

Mixed-Use, Market-Rate Rental

125 EAST 168TH STREET

Bronx, New York

Adaptive Reuse

128 FIFTH AVENUE

Brooklyn, New York

Mixed-Use, Market-Rate Rental, Retail

131 EAST 47TH STREET

New York, New York

Market-Rate Residential Condominium

132–138 EAST 45TH STREET

New York, New York

Adaptive Reuse, Recycled

137 CENTRE STREET

New York, New York

Market-Rate Residential Condominium

140 GROVE STREET

Stamford, Connecticut

Market-Rate Residential Condominium

Completed: 1965

145 CARROLL GARDENS

145 President Street

Brooklyn, New York

Market-Rate Residential Condominium

400 Fifth Avenue Residences (Langham Hotel)

145 EAST 76TH STREET
New York, New York
Market-Rate Residential Condominium
Completed: 1999

147 EAST 50TH STREET
New York, New York
Adaptive Reuse, Conversion

151 EAST 60TH STREET
New York, New York
Luxury Residential Condominium

157 BRUCE AVENUE
Yonkers, New York
Affordable Housing

160 EAST 84TH STREET
New York, New York
Market-Rate Residential Rental
Completed: 1963

165 EAST 35TH STREET
New York, New York
Market-Rate Residential
Completed: 1955

167 EAST 67TH STREET
New York, New York
Market-Rate Residential Condominium
Completed: 1960

167TH STREET
Bronx, New York
Adaptive Reuse, Rehabilitation

200 EAST 33RD STREET
New York, New York
Market-Rate Residential
Completed: pre-1971

210 WEST 102ND STREET
New York, New York
Affordable Housing
Completed: 2007

220 11TH AVENUE
New York, New York
Market-Rate Residential Condominium

235 EAST 14TH STREET
New York, New York
Affordable Housing
Completed: 1988

244 MADISON AVENUE
New York, New York
Adaptive Reuse, Recycled
Completed: 1970s

250 EAST 83RD STREET
New York, New York
Residential

301 EAST 80TH STREET
New York, New York
Market-Rate Residential Condominium

304 SPRING STREET
New York, New York
Market-Rate Residential Condominium
Completed: 2006

315 EAST 17TH STREET
New York, New York
Residential

320 EAST 58TH STREET
New York, New York
Market-Rate Residential Rental
Completed: 1961

330 WEST 56TH STREET
New York, New York
Market-Rate Residential Rental
Completed: 1974

345 EAST 56TH STREET
New York, New York
Market-Rate Residential Condominium
Completed: 1960

345 EAST 64TH STREET
New York, New York
Market-Rate Residential Rental
Completed: 1996

350 EAST 86TH STREET
New York, New York
Commercial, Theatre

350 WEST BROADWAY
New York, New York
Market-Rate Residential Condominium
Completed: 2008

360 LEXINGTON AVENUE
New York, New York
Commercial, Office Building
Completed: 1957

360 WEST 43RD STREET
New York, New York
Market-Rate Residential Rental
Completed: 2002

600 East 179th Street

368 THIRD AVENUE
New York, New York
Market-Rate Residential Rental
Completed: 1979

400 EAST 55TH STREET
New York, New York
Market-Rate Residential Rental
Completed: 1956

400 EAST 71ST STREET
New York, New York

400 FIFTH AVENUE RESIDENCES (LANGHAM HOTEL) (pictured p. 340)
New York, New York
Mixed-Use, Luxury Condominium, Hotel
Completed: 2010

401 EAST 65TH STREET
New York, New York

611 West 56th Street

Market-Rate Residential Rental

Completed: 1962

411 EAST 57TH STREET

New York, New York

Market-Rate Residential Condominium

Completed: 1959

420–424 WEST 20TH STREET

New York, New York

Adaptive Reuse, Conversion, Market-Rate Condominium

Completed: 2012

435 EAST 13TH STREET

New York, New York

Market-Rate Residential Rental

445 EAST 86TH STREET

New York, New York

Market-Rate Residential Rental

Completed: 1959

465 FIFTH AVENUE

New York, New York

Commercial, Office Building

Completed: 1970s

500 PARK AVENUE

New York, New York

530 WEST BROADWAY

Long Beach, New York

Market-Rate Residential Condominium

541 EAST 78TH STREET

New York, New York

Adaptive Reuse, Conversion

555 WEST 22ND STREET
New York, New York
Market-Rate Residential Condominium

575 MADISON AVENUE
New York, New York
Adaptive Reuse, Renovation
Completed: 2009

600 EAST 179TH STREET (pictured p. 341)
Bronx, New York
Senior Housing

611 WEST 56TH STREET (pictured p. 342)
New York, New York
Luxury Residential Condominium

681 FIFTH AVENUE
New York, New York
Adaptive Reuse, Restoration
Completed: 2010

702 SANSOM STREET
Philadelphia, Pennsylvania
Market-Rate Residential Condominium

710 EAST NINTH STREET
New York, New York
Adaptive Reuse, Conversion, Affordable Housing
Completed: 2013

764 LEXINGTON AVENUE
New York, New York
Completed: 1959

770 LEXINGTON AVENUE
New York, New York
Commercial, Office Building
Completed: 1960

777 SIXTH AVENUE
New York, New York
Market-Rate Residential Rental
Completed: 2001

810 RIVER AVENUE
Bronx, New York
Affordable Housing

815 FIFTH AVENUE
New York, New York
Market-Rate Residential Condominium

838 FIFTH AVENUE
New York, New York
Adaptive Reuse, Conversion

1170 OCEAN PARKWAY
Brooklyn, New York
Market-Rate Residential Condominium
Completed: 1965

1178 ANDERSON AVENUE
Bronx, New York
Affordable Housing
Completed: 2009

1214 FIFTH AVENUE
New York, New York
Luxury Residential Condominium, Medical Offices
Completed: 2012

1325 FIFTH AVENUE AT 112TH STREET
New York, New York
Affordable Housing
Completed: 1989

1330 FIFTH AVENUE AT 112TH STREET
New York, New York
Affordable Housing
Completed: 1989

1400 BROADWAY
New York, New York
Commercial, Office Building
Completed: 1970s

1600 BROADWAY ON THE SQUARE
New York, New York
Market-Rate Residential Condominium
Completed: 2007

1853 ANTHONY AVENUE
Bronx, New York
Affordable Housing
Completed: 2010

1865 SECOND AVENUE AT 96TH STREET
New York, New York
Affordable Housing
Completed: 1987

1920 WASHINGTON AVENUE AND EAST TREMONT AVENUE
Bronx, New York
Affordable Housing
Completed: 2008

1925 SECOND AVENUE
New York, New York
Market-Rate Residential Rental

A Condominiums

2035 NEWBOLD AVENUE
Bronx, New York
Affordable Housing

2049 RYER AVENUE
Bronx, New York
Affordable Supportive Housing

2051 RYER AVENUE
Bronx, New York
Affordable Housing

2500 JEROME AVENUE
Bronx, New York
Affordable Housing, Community

A CONDOMINIUMS (pictured left)
389 Washington Street
Jersey City, New Jersey
Market-Rate Residential Condominium
Completed: 2009

ABBEY VICTORIA GARAGE
133 West 51st Street
New York, New York
Commercial, Parking Garage
Completed: pre-1971

ADATH ISRAEL OF ASTORIA
36–02 14th Street
Astoria, New York
Public/Institutional, Synagogue
Completed: 1954

AHAVATH ISRAEL
108 Noble Street, Brooklyn, New York
Public/Institutional, Synagogue

AKA UNITED NATIONS
234 East 46th Street
New York, New York
Market-Rate Residential Rental
Completed: 1986

ALBERT EINSTEIN COLLEGE OF MEDICINE
– Athletic Complex & Labs
– Chanin Institute, Ullman Lab, Molecular Bio
– MRI Building
– Rousso Building
– Van Etten Clinical Skills Center
– Vin Lab (New Research Laboratory)
1300 Morris Park Avenue
Bronx, New York
Public/Institutional, Athletic Facilities
Completed: 1969–2004

ALL SAINTS HOUSING
53 East 131st Street
New York, New York
Affordable Housing
Completed: 2009

ALLENBY THE BAY (pictured p. 345)
2214–2222 Loretta Road
Far Rockaway, New York
Senior Living
Completed: 2013

ALTRO WORKSHOPS
Bronx, New York
Public/Institutional, Community
Completed: 1970s

AMERICAN MUSEUM OF NATURAL HISTORY (VARIOUS PROJECTS)
79th Street & Central Park West
New York, New York
Public/Institutional, Museum

AMERICAN STEEL PRODUCTS
Brooklyn, New York
Commercial, Office Building
Completed: 1970s

ANGEL GUARDIAN
261–263 Ninth Street
Brooklyn, New York
Adaptive Reuse, Rehabilitation
Completed: 2002

ANNA ERIKA
Staten Island, New York
Public/Institutional, Healthcare
Completed: pre-1981

ARC FT. WASHINGTON SENIOR CENTER

4111 Broadway

New York, New York

Senior Living

Completed: 2002

ARCHER AVENUE COMMUNITY HEALTHCARE CENTER FOR NEW YORK CITY HEALTH

166–10 Archer Avenue

Jamaica, New York

Public/Institutional, Hospital

ARMENIAN CHILDEN'S REHABILITATION CENTER*

Leninikan, Armenia

Healthcare, Pro-bono

Completed: 1989

ASTOR TERRACE

245 East 93rd Street

New York, New York

Market-Rate Residential

Condominium

Completed: 1986

ATLANTIC–COLUMBUS APARTMENTS

1675 Atlantic Avenue,

30 Columbus Place

Brooklyn, New York

Senior Living

AVALON AT GALLERY PLACE

770 Fifth Street NW

Washington, DC

Market-Rate Residential Rental

Completed: 2003

Allenby the Bay

The Bennett Condominium

AVALON MORNINGSIDE PARK
1 Morningside Drive
New York, New York
Market-Rate Residential Rental
Completed: 2008

THE AVERY
100 Riverside Drive South
New York, New York
Market-Rate Residential Condominium
Completed: 2007

BACCARAT HOTEL & RESIDENCES
28 East 53rd Street
New York, New York
Mixed-Use, Luxury Condominium, Hotel
Completed: 2015

BALDWIN JEWISH CENTER
Baldwin, New York
Public/Institutional, Synagogue

BANK OF NORTH AMERICA
36th Street and Eighth Avenue
New York, New York
Commercial, Bank
Completed: 1970s

BARRIER FREE LIVING
616 East 139th Street
Bronx, New York
Affordable Housing
Completed: 2015

BARUCH COLLEGE
New York, New York
Adaptive Reuse, Educational Facility
Completed: pre-1971

BAY TO BAY RESIDENTIAL CONDOMINIUM

Tampa, Florida

Market-Rate Residential Condominium

BAY TOWERS

319 Beach 98th Street

Rockaway Park, New York

Affordable Housing, Assisted Living

Completed: 1969

BAYSWATER JEWISH CENTER

2355 Healy Avenue

Far Rockaway, New York

Public/Institutional, Synagogue

Completed: 1959

BAYVIEW HOMES

Beach Channel and Seaside Avenue

Rockaway Park, New York

Affordable Housing

Completed: 2002

THE BEACON

54 Bristol Avenue, 445 Hopkinson Avenue

Brooklyn, New York

Affordable Housing

Completed: 2010

BELLEROSE SENIOR HOUSING

238-11 Hillside Avenue

Jamaica, New York

Senior Living

Completed: 1994

THE BENNETT CONDOMINIUM (pictured p.346)

786 West 187th Street

New York, New York

Market-Rate Condominium

Completed: 2005

BLOOMINGDALE'S

– New York, New York

– Stamford, Connecticut

Commercial, Retail

BOSTON SOUTH STATION

700 Atlantic Avenue

Boston, Massachusetts

Residential Interiors

THE BOULEVARD

2373 Broadway

New York, New York

Market-Rate Residential Condominium

Completed: 1987

BOULEVARD HOSPITAL

Long Island City, New York

Public/Institutional, Hospital

Completed: 1970s

BRANCH MOTORS

Brooklyn, New York

Commercial, Office Building

Completed: 1970s

BRITISH AIRWAYS

Broad Street

New York, New York

Commercial, Office Building

BROAD STREET – NOBU HOTEL

New York, New York

Hospitality, Hotel

BRONX CARE HOUSING

1664 Morris Avenue

Bronx, New York

Affordable/Low-Income Housing

Completed: 2007

BRONX–LEBANON HOSPITAL CENTER

2432 Grand Concourse

Bronx, New York

Public/Institutional, Hospital

BROOKDALE SENIORS RESIDENCE

560 Rockaway Parkway

Brooklyn, New York

Senior Living

Completed: 1998

BROOKLYN EYE AND EAR HOSPITAL

Brooklyn, New York

Adaptive Reuse, Conversion

THE BROWNING SCHOOL FOR BOYS

New York, New York

Public/Institutional, Education Facility

BUNNIES DEPARTMENT STORE

Delancey Street

New York, New York

Commercial, Retail/Shopping Center

BURNDY CORPORATION

– Bethel, Connecticut

– Orange, Connecticut

Commercial, Office Building

Completed: 1970s

CALYER PLACE

27–41 West Street

Brooklyn, New York

Market-Rate Residential Rental

THE CARAVELLE
445 East 86th Street
New York, New York
Market-Rate Residential Condominium
Completed: 1961

CARLTON HOUSE
35 North Chatsworth Avenue
Larchmont, New York
Market-Rate Residential Rental
Completed: 1995

CARLTON HOUSE/PLAZA
26 Strawberry Hill Avenue
Stamford, Connecticut
Residential
Completed: 1980

CARMEL RICHMOND-PACE
Park Avenue
Staten Island, New York
Senior Living, Assisted Living
Completed: 2011

CARNEGIE HOUSE
100 West 57th Street
New York, New York
Residential
Completed: 1962

CARRIAGE HOUSE
510 East 80th Street
New York, New York
Market-Rate Residential Condominium
Completed: 1986

CASABLANCA (pictured p. 349)
121–125 East 110th Street
New York, New York
Affordable Housing
Completed: 2009

CASITA PARK
100 East 112th Street
New York, New York
Senior Living
Completed: 2002

CASA 74
255 East 74th Street
New York, New York
Luxury Residential Condominium
Completed: 2009

CASTLETON MANOR SENIOR HOUSING
35 Gordon Street
Staten Island, New York
Senior Living
Completed: 2001

CATHOLIC CHARITIES – HOUSING FOR THE HOMELESS
Willoughby Avenue
Brooklyn, New *York*
Affordable Housing

CENTRAL SYNAGOGUE – NEW YORK
652 Lexington Avenue
New York, New York
Public/Institutional, Synagogue

CENTRAL SYNAGOGUE – ROCKVILLE CENTRE
Rockville Centre, New York
Public/Institutional, Synagogue

THE CENTRALE
138 East 50th Street
New York, New York
Market-Rate Residential Condominium

CHAREL HOUSE
80th Street and Madison Avenue
New York, New York

THE CHARLESTON
225 East 34th Street
New York, New York
Market-Rate Residential Condominium
Completed: 2007

THE CHATHAM
108–25 72nd Avenue
Forest Hills, New York
Residential
Completed: 1959

CHELSEA ATELIER
245 Seventh Avenue
New York, New York
Adaptive Reuse, Conversion
Completed: 1997

CHELSEA ENCLAVE
177 Ninth Avenue
New York, New York
Luxury Residential Condominium
Completed: 2010

CINEPLEX ODEON CINEMA
New York, New York
Commercial

CHICAGO EXPRESS
Brooklyn, New York

Casablanca

Commercial, Office Building

Completed: 1970s

THE CLAREMONT

1421 College Avenue,

East 171st Street

Bronx, New York

Senior Living

Completed: 2010

THE CLAYTON WILLIAMS RESIDENCE

620–630 Concord Avenue

Bronx, New York

Affordable/Supportive Housing

CNR SENIOR HOUSING

80 Lefferts Place

Brooklyn, New York

Senior Living

CO-OP CITY

Bronx, New York

Public/Institutional, Nursing Home

COFFEE INSTANTS

Queens, New York

Commercial, Office Building

Completed: 1970s

THE COLLEGE OF STATEN ISLAND

Staten Island, New York

Public/Institutional, Education Facility, University

COLUMBIA UNIVERSITY

– Leroy Neiman Gallery and Lobby, Dodge Hall

– Faculty and Graduate Housing

New York, New York

Public/Institutional, Education Facility

COLUMBUS SQUARE

801 Amsterdam

New York, New York

Market-Rate Residential Rental

Completed: 2009

COMMUNITY NATIONAL BANK

Staten Island, New York

Commercial, Bank

Completed: 1970s

COMMUNITY HOSPITAL OF BROOKLYN

Brooklyn, New York

Public/Institutional, Hospital

Completed: 1970s

COMMUNITY SYNAGOGUE

Rye, New York

Public/Institutional, Synagogue

Completed: 1959

Crown Building

THE CONCERTO
200 West 60th Street
New York, New York
Market-Rate Residential Rental
Completed: 1991

CONGREGATION BETH SHOLOM
390 Broadway
Lawrence, New York
Public/Institutional, Synagogue
Completed: 1950

CONGREGATION CZERNOWITZ-BUKOVINER
New York
Public/Institutional, Synagogue
Completed: 1952

CONGREGATION SHAARAY TEFILA
25 Central Avenue
Lawrence, New York
Public/Institutional, Synagogue

COTTAGE PLACE GARDENS
188 Warburton Avenue
Yonkers, New York
Affordable Housing

COURTLANDT COMMUNITY
929 Courtlandt Street
Bronx, New York
Affordable/Supportive Housing
Completed: 2012

CRESTHAVEN RETIREMENT COMMUNITY
150th Street and Powells Cove Boulevard
Flushing, New York
Senior Living

THE CROSSROADS
10 Rutgers Street and East Broadway
New York, New York
Market-Rate Residential Rental
Completed: 2000

CROWN BUILDING (pictured p. 350)
730 Fifth Avenue
New York, New York
Adaptive Reuse, Luxury Condominium

D & D BUILDING
979 Third Avenue
New York, New York
Commercial, Retail

DAVID MINKIN NURSING HOME AT KINGSBROOK MEDICAL CENTER
Ninth Avenue between 53rd and 54th Streets
Brooklyn, New York
Senior Living, Senior Housing
Completed: 1996

DAVIDSON APARTMENTS
1750 Davidson Avenue
Bronx, New York
Affordable Housing
Completed: 2007

DEEPDALE GENERAL HOSPITAL
Littleneck, New York
Healthcare
Completed: 1970s

DEUTSCHETELEKOM
New York, New York

DIOCESE OF BROOKLYN
310 Prospect Park West
Brooklyn, New York
Adaptive Reuse, Conversion
Completed: 2000

DOCTORS HOSPITAL
170 East End Avenue
New York, New York
Healthcare
Completed: 1980s

LE DOMAINE
403 East 62nd Street
New York, New York
Market-Rate Residential Condominium
Completed: 1985

DREITZER HOUSE
323–329 East 155th Street
New York, New York
Affordable Housing
Completed: 1999

DRY DOCK SAVINGS BANK
– 38th Street and Eighth Avenue
– 59th Street and Lexington Avenue
– 60 East 42nd Street
– 60th Street
– 512 Seventh Avenue
– 555 Seventh Avenue
– 770 Third Avenue
– 1270 Lexington Avenue
– 1340 Third Avenue
– Delancey Street
– Grand Street
– Hicksville, New York
– Katonah, New York
– Merrick Road, Rockville Center, New York
– Queens Boulevard, Queens, New York
– White Plains, New York
Commercial, Bank
Completed: 1970s

EAST SIDE SUITES
New York, New York
Completed: 1960–1962

EGER HARBOR HOUSE
110 Meiser Avenue
Staten Island, New York
Affordable Housing
Completed: 2004

ELIJAH SMITH RESIDENCE
385 Throop Avenue
Brooklyn, New York
Senior Living
Completed: 1998

ELMONT JEWISH CENTER
500 Elmont Road
Elmont, New York
Public/Institutional, Synagogue

ELMONT MULTIPLEX THEATRES
Commercial, Theatre

ELTON STREET
Spring Creek
Brooklyn, New York
Senior Living

THE EMPIRE
188 East 78th Street
New York, New York
Mixed-Use, Rehabilitation, Market-Rate Rentals

EMPIRE HOUSE
200 East 70th Street

Friendly Hands Apartments

New York, New York

Market-Rate Residential Rental

Completed: 1961

ENZO BIO CHEM

New York, New York

Public/Institutional,
Research Facility

EPISCOPAL CHURCH HOUSING, PILOT COVE

City Island

Bronx, New York

Affordable Housing

ERASMUS HIGH SCHOOL

911 Flatbush Avenue

Brooklyn, New York

Public/Institutional, Education Facility

ESSEX CROSSING SITE 1

242 Broome Street

New York, New York

Market-Rate Residential Condominium

EUGENE SMILOVIC ARMS

280 East 170th Street

Bronx, New York

Senior Living

Completed: 1996

EVELYN AND LOUIS GREEN RESIDENCE

200 East Fifth Street

New York, New York

Market-Rate Residential

Completed: 1985

EXCALIBUR ARMS

Freeport, Grand Bahama Island

Commercial, Hotel

Completed: pre-1981

EXCELSIOR 11

Nelson Avenue and West 169th Street

Bronx, New York

Affordable/Supportive Housing

EXCELUM ALUMINUM

Plainview, New York

Commercial, Office Building

Completed: 1970s

FALCON TOWERS

245 East 44th Street

New York, New York

Market-Rate Residential Rental

Completed: 1987

FANNIE LOU HAMER SENIOR HOUSING

1181 1186 Walton Avenue

Bronx, New York

Senior Living

Completed: 1993

FAWCETT BUILDING

New York, New York

Commercial, Office Building

Completed: 1970s

FIRST FEDERAL SAVINGS & LOAN ASSOC.

- 30 East 65th Street
- 72nd Street
- 1530 Unionport Road (Bronx)
- 2690 Victory Boulevard (Staten Island)
- Rockefeller Plaza

Commercial, Bank

Completed: 1970s

FLATBUSH GENERAL HOSPITAL
Brooklyn, New York
Healthcare
Completed: 1970s

FLORA VISTA SUPPORTIVE HOUSING
326–330 East 116th Street
New York, New York
Affordable/Supportive Housing
Completed: 2005

FOREST CITY DALY
– Jericho, New York
– Roslyn, New York
Senior/Assisted Living

FOUNTAIN HILL NURSING HOME
Bethlehem, New York
Public/Institutional, Nursing Home

FRANKLIN AVENUE APARTMENTS
1363 Franklin Avenue
Bronx, New York
Affordable/Supportive Housing
Completed: 2005

FRIENDLY HANDS APARTMENTS
(pictured p. 352)
225 East 118th Street
New York, New York
Affordable Housing
Completed: 2009

FRIENDLY TOWERS
1262 Nelson Avenue
Bronx, New York
Affordable/Supportive Housing
Completed: 2008

FT. HAMILTON HIGH SCHOOL (MODULAR TEMPORARY CLASSROOMS)
8301 Shore Road
Brooklyn, New York
Public/Institutional, Education Facility
Completed: 1991

FULLER BRUSH COMPANY
Brooklyn, New York
Commercial, Office Building
Completed: 1970s

GARDEN MANOR SENIOR HOUSING
250 Park Avenue South
Staten Island, New York
Senior Living
Completed: 1995

GENESIS
113 East 13th Street
New York, New York

GENESIS II
350 Snediker Avenue
Brooklyn, New York
Affordable Housing
Completed: 2011

GEORGE T. DOURIS
35–03 29th Street, Astoria Boulevard
Astoria, New York
Senior Living
Completed: 2009

GERARD AVENUE APARTMENTS
Bronx, New York
Affordable Housing
Completed: early 1990s

GLOUCESTER APARTMENTS
200 West 79th Street
New York, New York
Market-Rate Residential Condominium
Completed: 1976

GOUVERNEUR PLACE APARTMENTS
450–548 Gouverneur Place
Bronx, New York
Affordable Housing
Completed: 2016

GRAND MILLENNIUM LINCOLN WEST
1965 Broadway
New York, New York
Market-Rate Residential Condominium
Completed: 1997

GRAND STREET SETTLEMENT
706–717 East 6th Street
New York, New York
Senior Living
Completed: 2004

GROSVENOR HOUSE
22 West 15th Street
New York, New York
Market-Rate Residential Condominium
Completed: 1989

GUN HILL ROAD IMAGING CENTER
Bronx, New York
Public/Institutional, Hospital
Completed: 1997

H.I.P. YORKVILLE MEDICAL CENTER
160 East 84th Street
New York, New York

Highgrove

Hospital

Completed: 1970s

THE HANLEY

165 East 66th Street

New York, New York

Residential

Completed: 1957

HARDROCK HOTEL

159 West 48th Street

New York, New York

Hospitality, Hotel

HARTSDALE APARTMENTS

Hartsdale, New York

Residential

Completed: 1970s

HAVERSTRAW PLACE

Route 9W Village of Haverstraw

Rockland County, New York

Senior Living

Completed: 2001

HEBREW HOSPITAL FOR THE CHRONIC SICK

Bronx, New York

Healthcare

Completed: 1970s

HEROLD ELECTRONICS

Bronx, New York

Commercial, Office Building

Completed: 1970s

HIGHBRIDGE SENIOR HOUSING

1430 Plimpton Avenue

Bronx, New York

Senior Living

Completed: 2005

HIGHGROVE (pictured left)

70 Forest Street

Stamford, Connecticut

Market-Rate Residential Condominium

Design Architect: Robert A.M. Stern Architects

Completed: 2009

HIGHLINE 310

New York, New York

Hospitality, Hotel

THE HILARY GARDENS

300 Mercer Street

New York, New York

Residential

Completed: 1976

HILCREST JEWISH CENTER

Flushing, New York

Public/Institutional, Synagogue

Completed: 1970s

HOLY SPIRIT

17th Avenue and 47th Street

Brooklyn, New York

Senior Living

Completed: 1992

HOSPITAL FOR JOINT DISEASES

301 East 17th Street

New York, New York

Public/Institutional, Hospital

Completed: 1980s

HUDSON RESIDENCES

515 West 18th Street and

555 West 22nd Street

New York, New York

Luxury Residential Condominium

HUDSON TEA – BUILDING "A"

1500 Hudson Street

Hoboken, New Jersey

Market-Rate Residential Condominium

Completed: 2005–2007

HUNTER'S POINT SOUTH – PARCEL C SOUTH TOWER

52–1 through 52–99 Second Street

Long Island City, New York

Affordable Housing

HAYM SALOMAN HOME FOR AGED

Brooklyn, New York

Public/Institutional, Adult Healthcare

HYGIENE SHOWER CURTAIN

Brooklyn, New York

Commercial, Office Building

Completed: 1970s

IMPERIAL HOUSE

125 Prospect Street

Stamford, Connecticut

Residential

Completed: 1980

INDEPENDENT ENRICHED SENIOR HOUSING

45–02 Ditmars Boulevard

Astoria, New York

Adaptive Reuse, Conversion, Senior Housing

INKWELL (pictured right)

520 West 45th Street

New York, New York

Adaptive Reuse, Conversion, Market-Rate Condominium

Completed: 2016

INTERNATIONAL SERVICE EMPLOYEES UNION HEALTH CENTER

New York, New York

Public/Institutional, Hospital

Completed: 1970s

ISABELLA SENIOR HOUSING

515 Audubon Avenue

New York, New York

Public/Institutional, Nursing Home, Renovation

IVY HILL LITHOGRAPHY

Brooklyn, New York

Commercial, Office Building

Completed: 1970s

IVY TOWER (pictured p. 356)

350 West 43rd Street

New York, New York

Market-Rate Residential Rental

Completed: 2003

JACKSON EAST

26–32 Jackson Avenue

Long Island City, New York

Mixed-Use, Market-Rate Residential, Retail

JAMAICA CENTER RETAIL AND CINEMA

Commercial, Cinema

Completed: 1996–2001

Inkwell

JAMAICA HOSPITAL
8900 Van Wyck Expressway
Richmond Hill, New York
Healthcare
Completed: 1970s

JAMAICA SENIOR HOUSING
89–05 134th Street
Jamaica, New York
Senior Living

Ivy Tower

JAMES SQUARE HEALTH & REHAB
918 James Street
Syracuse, New York
Public/Institutional, Nursing Home

JASA REGIONAL HEADQUARTERS
161 Corbin Place
Brooklyn, New York

JASMINE COURT
East 147th Street and Brook
Bronx, New York
Affordable/Supportive Housing

JBG AIDS–SNF
Yonkers, New York
Public/Institutional, Nursing Home

JENNIFER TOWER
330 East 39th Street
New York, New York
Market-Rate Residential
Completed: pre-1981

JEWISH ASSOCIATION SERVICES FOR THE AGED
Brooklyn, New York
Affordable Housing

JEWISH COMMUNITY CENTER OF HARRISON
Harrison, New York
Public/Institutional, Synagogue
Completed: 1959

JEWISH GUILD FOR THE BLIND (GUILD CARE)
– Buffalo, New York
– New York, New York
– Syracuse, New York
Public/Institutional, Adult Healthcare

JEWISH HOME LIFECARE-ZWEIG
Adaptive Reuse, Conversion
Completed: 2014

JOYVA WAREHOUSE
Brooklyn, New York
Commercial
Completed: pre-1981

JUDITH LYNN HEALTH FACILITY
Bronx, New York
Public/Institutional, Healthcare
Completed: 1970s

JUNIOR HIGH SCHOOL 252
Brooklyn, New York
Public/Institutional, Education Facility

THE KENMORE HOTEL
145 East 23rd Street
New York, New York
Adaptive Reuse, Conversion, Affordable Housing
Completed: 1999

KENTON
333 Bowery
New York, New York
Affordable/Low-Income Housing
Completed: 1995

THE KENTON PLACE
305 East 63rd Street
New York, New York
Adaptive Reuse, Conversion, Luxury Condominium

KEY WEST/WEST 96TH

750 Columbus Avenue

New York, New York

Market-Rate Residential Rental

Completed: 1988

KFI FOOD DISTRIBUTORS

Bronx, New York

Commercial, Office Building

Completed: 1970s

KINGS HIGHWAY HOSPITAL

Brooklyn, New York

Public/Institutional, Hospital

Completed: 1970s

KNESES ISRAEL

Brooklyn, New York

Public/Institutional, Synagogue

THE KNICKERBOCKER

308 East 72nd Street

New York, New York

Residential

Completed: 1980s

KORVETTES DEPARTMENT STORE

Delancey Street

New York, New York

Commercial, Retail/Shopping Center

KRASDALE FOODS, INC

New York, New York

KURT & LEAH SCHNEIDER APARTMENTS

West 102nd Street

New York, New York

Senior Living

Completed: 1999

The Larstrand

LA GUARDIA COMMUNITY COLLEGE

Long Island City, New York

Public/Institutional, Education Facility, University

LACK CARPET COMPANY

Brooklyn, New York

Commercial, Office Building

Completed: 1970s

LADY QUEEN OF MARTYRS PRIEST RETIREMENT CENTER

72nd Road & Queens Boulevard

Forest Hills, New York

Supportive Housing

Completed: 2003

THE LARA

113 Nassau Street

New York, New York

Market-Rate Residential Rental

Completed: 2013

LARCHMONT TEMPLE

Larchmont, New York

The Maximillian

Public/Institutional, Synagogue

THE LARSTRAND (pictured p. 357)

227 West 77th Street

New York, New York

Market-Rate Residential Rental

Completed: 2013

THE LAUREL

400 East 67th Street

New York, New York

Market-Rate Residential Condominium

Completed: 2005

THE LAURENCE TOWERS

200 East 33rd Street

New York, New York

Market-Rate Residential Rental

Completed: 1972

LENOX HOUSE APARTMENTS

301 East 78th Street

New York, New York

Completed: 1963

LEXINGTON PARC

127 East 30th Street

New York, New York

Market-Rate Residential Condominium

Completed: 1988

LIBERTY VILLAGE

250 Liberty Street

Plainfield, New Jersey

Affordable Housing

LINCOLN TRIANGLE

1960 Broadway

New York, New York

Market-Rate Residential Rental

Completed: 1995

LINDEN HOUSE

41 Hope Street

Stamford, Connecticut

Residential

Completed: 1970s

LITTLE SISTERS OF THE POOR

Brooklyn, New York

Affordable Housing

LOCAL 32 B/J BUILDING SERVICE UNION HEALTH CENTER

New York, New York

Public/Institutional, Hospital

Completed: 1970s

LOEWS CINEMA

– Kips Bay, 70 Second Avenue

– Rio Washingtonian, Gathersburg, Maryland

– Elmurst, New York

– Lincoln Square, New York

Commercial, Cinema

Completed: 1995–1998

LONGACRE HOUSE

305 West 50th Street

New York, New York

Market-Rate Residential Rental

Completed: 1997

LONG ISLAND CARE CENTER

Long Island, New York

Public/Institutional, Hospital

LONG ISLAND COLLEGE HOSPITAL

339 Hicks Street

Brooklyn, New York

Healthcare

Completed: 1970s

LONG ISLAND EYE SURGERY CENTER

Long Island, New York

Public/Institutional, Hospital

LOUISE CHAZIN APARTMENTS

125 East 168th Street

Bronx, New York

Affordable Housing

LOVELY HILLS

Pawling, New York

Public/Institutional, Healthcare

Completed: pre-1981

LUCILLE CLARK HOUSING FOR THE ELDERLY

244–252 West 112th Street

New York, New York

Senior Living

Completed: 2002

LYDIA E. HALL HOSPITAL

Freeport, New York

Public/Institutional, Hospital

Completed: 1970s

MAIMONEDES MEDICAL CENTER

4802 Tenth Avenue

Brooklyn, New York

Hospital

MAMARONECK AVENUE TOWERS

76 Mamaroneck Avenue

White Plains, New York

Mixed-Use, Market-Rate Residential Rental, Retail

MANDALAY ON THE HUDSON

20 Second Street

Jersey City, New Jersey

Market-Rate Residential Condominium

Completed: 2000

MANHATTAN ATHLETIC CLUB

277 Park Avenue

New York, New York

Hospitality, Athletic Facilities

Completed: 2001

MANHATTAN BOWERY – R.C.C.A. – CAFETERIA

New York, New York

Public/Institutional, Supportive Housing

MANHATTAN DAY SCHOOL

New York, New York

Public/Institutional, Education Facility

Completed: 1970s

MANHATTAN HEBREW HIGH SCHOOL

Riverdale, New York

Public/Institutional, Education Facility

MANHATTAN VALLEY RESTORATION CORPORATION

Columbus Avenue and 108th Street

New York, New York

Affordable Housing

MANUFACTURERS HANOVER TRUST CO.

Fountain and Loring Avenues

Brooklyn, New York

Commercial

Completed: 1970s

THE MARAIS

520 West 23rd Street

New York, New York

Market-Rate Residential Rental

Completed: 2003

MARYMOUNT COLLEGE DORM

New York, New York

Public/Institutional, Education Facility

THE MAXIMILIAN (pictured p. 358)

5–11 47th Avenue

Long Island City, New York

Market-Rate Residential Rental

Completed: 2014

MELVILLE GARDENS

Huntington, New York

Senior/Assisted Living

MESIVTA OHR TORAH HIGH SCHOOL

Riverdale, New York

Public/Institutional, Education Facility

Completed: 1970s

METROPOLITAN JEWISH GERIATRIC NURSING HOME

4915 Tenth Avenue

Brooklyn, New York

Public/Institutional, Nursing Home

THE METRO

301 West 53rd Street

New York, New York

The Metropolitan

Market-Rate Residential Condominium

Completed: 1980

THE METROPOLITAN (pictured above)

181 East 90th Street

New York, New York

Luxury Residential Condominium

Completed: 2003

METROPOLITAN HOSPITAL

New York, New York

Public/Institutional, Hospital

Completed: pre-1971

MIDDLETOWN PLAZA SHOPPING CENTER

Middletown, New Jersey

Commercial, Retail/Shopping Center

Completed: pre-1981

MIDWOOD HIGH SCHOOL (MODULAR CLASSROOMS)

2839 Bedford Avenue

Brooklyn, New York

Public/Institutional, Education Facility

MILAGROSA HOUSING

177 East 101st Street

New York, New York

Adaptive Reuse, Conversion

THE MONARCH

200 East 89th Street

New York, New York

Market-Rate Residential Condominium

Completed: 1987

THE MONTEREY

4278–4284 Third Avenue

Bronx, New York

Affordable Housing

Completed: 2008

MOSES HOSPITAL

Bronx, New York

Public/Institutional, Hospital

Completed: 1996

MOST HOLY TRINITY

157 Graham Avenue

Brooklyn, New York

Adaptive Reuse, Rehabilitation

Completed: 2009

MOUNT CARMEL MONASTERY

715 St. Johns Place

Brooklyn, New York

Adaptive Reuse, Conversion, Senior Housing

Completed: 2003

MOUNT CARMEL SENIOR HOUSING

745 St. Johns Place

Brooklyn, New York

Senior Living

Completed: 2003

MOUNT PLEASANT APARTMENTS

421–435 East 116th Street

New York, New York

Senior Living

Completed: 1997

MOUNT PLEASANT MEADOWS SMITHTOWN

Smithtown, New York

Senior/Assisted Living

MOUNT VERNON HOUSING

Mount Vernon, New York

Affordable Housing

MSGR. EDWARD T. BURKE

East Eighth Street, Parkville and Newkirk Avenue

Brooklyn, New York

Senior Living

Completed: 1992

MSGR. JOSEPH F. STEDMAN SENIOR APARTMENTS

930 53rd Street

Brooklyn, New York

Senior Living

Completed: 2000

MORRISTOWN MOVING FORWARD
250 Spring Street
Morristown, New Jersey
Mixed-Use, Hotel, Residential Rental

MT. CALVARY APARTMENTS
100 Chadwick Avenue
Newark, New Jersey
Residential
Completed: 1970s

MT. SINAI WEST
425 West 59th Street
New York, New York
Hospital

MYRTLE AVENUE APARTMENTS
853 Myrtle Avenue
Brooklyn, New York
Affordable Housing
Completed: 2007

NANCY DESGROTTES APARTMENTS
106 Gerry Street, East Williamsburg
Brooklyn, New York
Affordable/Low-Income Housing
Completed: 2001

NATIONAL AMUSEMENTS THEATRES
Jamaica, New York
Commercial, Theater

NEW HYDE PARK MEDICAL CENTER
New Hyde Park, New York
Healthcare
Completed: 1970s

THE NEW JEWISH HOME
2553 University Avenue
Bronx, New York
Senior/Assisted Living
Completed: 2013

NEW PROVIDENCE SHELTER
215–225 East 45th Street
New York, New York
Adaptive Reuse, Renovation, Low-Income Housing
Completed: 1998

NEW ROCHELLE HOSPITAL MEDICAL CENTER
New York, New York
Public/Institutional, Research Facility

THE NEW THEATRE BUILDING
240 East Tenth Street
New York, New York
Market-Rate Residential Condominium
Completed: 2001

NEW YORK HEALTH & RACQUET CLUB (5 LOCATIONS)
New York, New York
Public/Institutional, Athletic Facilities

NEW YORK LAW SCHOOL
New York, New York
Public/Institutional, Education Facility

NEW YORK TELEPHONE COMPANY
New York, New York
Commercial

NEW YORK TOWER
330 East 39th Street
New York, New York
Luxury Residential Condominium
Completed: 1982

NEW YORK UNIVERSITY HOSPITAL
New York, New York
Public/Institutional, Hospital

NEWTON INDUSTRIAL CENTER
Brooklyn, New York
Commercial, Office Building
Completed: 1970s

NORTH CENTRAL BRONX HOSPITAL
Bronx, New York
Public/Institutional, Hospital
Completed: pre-1971

NYSCO PHARMACY
Queens, New York
Commercial, Office Building
Completed: 1970s

NURSING HOME – SYRACUSE
Syracuse, New York
Senior/Assisted Living
Completed: 1970

OAKLAND JEWISH CENTER
Bayside, New York
Public/Institutional, Synagogue

OCEANSIDE JEWISH CENTER
Oceanside, New York
Public/Institutional, Synagogue

ONE BEEKMAN STREET (pictured p. 362)
New York, New York

One Beekman Street

Design Architect: Richard Rogers

Market-Rate Residential Condominium

ONE COLUMBUS PLACE

400 West 59th Street

New York, New York

ONE FLUSHING

133–45 41st Avenue

Flushing, New York

Affordable Housing

ONE JAMAICA CENTER

Jamaica Avenue and Archer Avenue

Jamaica, New York

Commercial, Cinema, Retail

ONE LINCOLN SQUARE

150 Columbus Avenue

New York, New York

Market-Rate Residential Condominium

Completed: 1995

ONE WEST 34TH STREET

New York, New York

Commercial, Office Building

Completed: 1970s

OUR LADY OF MERCY MEDICAL CENTER

4168–4170 Carpenter Avenue

Bronx, New York

Senior Living

Completed: 1997

OUR LADY OF MERCY MANOR

640 East 232nd Street

Bronx, New York

Senior Living

Completed: 2001

OUR LADY QUEEN OF MARTYRS
109–04 72nd Road
Forest Hills, New York
Adaptive Reuse, Rehabilitation, Community
Completed: 2003

OVINGTON MANOR
Brooklyn, New York
Public/Insitutional, Healthcare
Completed: pre-1981

OXFORD AVENUE APARTMENTS
3625–3629 Oxford Avenue
Bronx, New York
Market-Rate Residential Rental
Completed: 2004

PACE UNIVERSITY – MODERNIZATION
New York, New York
Adaptive Reuse

PALM BEACH HOME FOR ADULTS
2900 Bragg Street
Brooklyn, New York
Public/Institutional, Adult Healthcare

PALM GARDENS HOME FOR ADULTS
615 Avenue C
Brooklyn, New York
Public/Institutional, Nursing Home

PALM TREE NURSING HOME
5606 15th Avenue
Brooklyn, New York
Public/Institutional, Nursing Home

PALMER HOUSE
609 Palmer Road
Yonkers, New York
Affordable Housing

THE PARC
Queens, New York
Completed: 1959

THE PARIS
752 West End Avenue
New York, New York
Adaptive Reuse, Luxury Condominium

PARK AVENUE SYNAGOGUE
New York, New York
Public/Institutional, Synagogue

PARK COLUMBUS
101 West 87th Street
New York, New York
Adaptive Reuse, Conversion, Market-Rate Condominium
Completed: 2013

PARK SOUTH TOWER
124 West 60th Street
New York, New York
Market-Rate Residential Rental
Completed: 1986

PARK WILLOW – BUILDINGS H AND I
Hoboken, New Jersey
Mixed-Use, Market-Rate Condominium

PARKSIDE TERRACE
3211 Parkside Place
Bronx, New York
Affordable Housing

PARKVILLE SENIOR CITIZENS HOUSING
720 East Eighth Street
Brooklyn, New York
Affordable Housing

PAYTON LANE RESIDENTIAL CARE FACILITY
Southampton, New York
Public/Institutional, Adult Healthcare

THE PEARL
400 East 66th Street
New York, New York
Market-Rate Residential Rental
Completed: 1999

PELHAM PARKWAY JEWISH CENTER
Bronx, New York
Public/Institutional, Synagogue

PERMANENT MISSION OF THE PEOPLE'S REPUBLIC OF CHINA TO THE UNITED NATIONS
350 East 35th Street
New York, New York

PETITE FLEUR NURSING HOME
300 Broadway Avenue
Sayville, New York
Public/Institutional, Nursing Home

PHIPPS HOUSING
325 East 25th Street
New York, New York
Affordable Housing

PIERREPONT HOUSING
55 Pierrepont Street

Brooklyn, New York
Affordable Housing

PLYMOUTH TOWER
349 East 92nd Street
New York, New York
Market-Rate Residential Condominium
Completed: 1977

THE POINTE
South Fourth Avenue & Third Street
Mount Vernon, New York
Affordable Housing

POPPENHUSEN LIBRARY
121–23 14th Avenue
College Point, New York
Public/Institutional, Restoration, Library
Completed: 2003

PORTOFINO (pictured p. 365)
1 Second Street
Jersey City, New Jersey
Market-Rate Residential Condominium
Completed: 2005

POSITIVELY 3RD STREET
306–312 East Third Street
New York, New York
Senior Living
Completed: 2006

LE PREMIER
112 West 56th Street
New York, New York
Completed: 1983

PRESBYTERIAN SENIOR SERVICES
106th Street and Amsterdam
New York, New York
Affordable Housing

PRINCETON HOUSE
231 West 95th Street
New York, New York
Market-Rate Residential Condominium
Completed: 1986

PS–3
Yonkers, New York
Adaptive Reuse, Conversion

PS–51, PS–52, PS–55, PS–69, PS–72, PS–76, IS–72, IS–51, PS–85, PS–190, PS–101
City-Wide
New York, New York
Public/Institutional, Education Facility

QUINCY STREET RESIDENCE
625 Quincy Street
Brooklyn, New York
Senior Living
Completed: 2006

RAMAZ SCHOOL – GRADES K–12
14th Street
New York, New York
Public/Institutional, Education Facility

RAYMOND RANCH HOMES
Rockville Centre, New York
Completed: 1951

RED SQUARE
250 East Houston Street
New York, New York
Market-Rate Residential Rental
Completed: 1989

THE REMBRANDT
31 Jane Street
New York, New York
Residential
Completed: 1962

THE RICHMOND
201 East 80th Street
New York, New York
Market-Rate Residential Condominium
Completed: 1994

RICHMOND GARDENS
247 Jersey Street
Staten Island, New York
Affordable Housing

RITZ PLAZA
235 West 48th Street
New York, New York
Market-Rate Residential Rental
Completed: 1989

RIVER EAST
408 East 92nd Street
New York, New York
Market-Rate Residential Rental
Completed: 2005

RIVER TERRACE
515 East 72nd Street
New York, New York
Market-Rate Residential Condominium
Completed: 1985

Portofino

RIVERBANK WEST

560 West 43rd Street

New York, New York

Market-Rate Residential Rental

Completed: 1987

RIVERDALE HOUSING FOR THE ELDERLY

Broadway and Mosholu Avenue

Bronx, New York

Senior Living

Completed: 1998

RIVERHILL APARTMENTS

185 Van Rensselaer Boulevard

Albany, New York

Residential

Completed: 1970s

RIVERCOURT

429 East 52nd Street

New York, New York

Market-Rate Residential Rental

Completed: 1974

RIVERTOWER

415 East 53rd Street/Sutton Place

at 54th Street

New York, New York

Market-Rate Residential Rental

Completed: 1982

RIVERWATCH

70 Battery Place

New York, New York

Market-Rate Residential Rental

Completed: 1998

RIVINGTON

New York, New York

Adaptive Reuse, Conversion

ROCKEFELLER CENTER COMPLEX

(Window Replacement Program)

Rockefeller Center

New York, New York

Landmark

Completed: 2006–2008

ROCKEFELLER UNIVERSITY HOSPITAL

1230 York Avenue

New York, New York

Healthcare

Completed: 1970s

RODNEY VILLAGE SHOPPING CENTER

Dover, Delaware

Commercial, Retail/Shopping Center

Completed: pre-1981

ROGERS DRUG COMPANY
Lindenhurst, New York
Commercial, Office Building
Completed: 1970s

RONALD MCDONALD HOUSE
New York, New York
Public/Institutional, Community
Completed: 2010

ROOSEVELT MALL NORTHEAST
Philadelphia, Pennsylvania
Commercial, Retail/Shopping Center
Completed: pre-1971

ROSARY HOUSE SENIOR APARTMENTS (OUR LADY OF FATIMA)
30th Avenue between 78th and 79th Streets
Astoria, New York
Senior Living
Completed: 1997

THE ROYAL ELIZABETH
80 Elizabeth Street
New York, New York
Adaptive Reuse, Conversion

ROYAL NATIONAL BANK, WILLIAMSBURG
Brooklyn, New York
Commercial, Bank
Completed: 1970s

THE ROYALE
188 East 64th Street
New York, New York
Market-Rate Residential Condominium
Completed: 1987

RUGGED CROSS APARTMENTS
12 Patchen Avenue and Lafayette Avenue
Brooklyn, New York
Affordable/Supportive Housing
Completed: 2008

RYE COMMUNITY CENTER
Rye, New York
Public/Insitutional, Community
Completed: pre-1981

THE SAGAMORE
189 West 89th Street
New York, New York
Market-Rate Residential Rental
Completed: 1997

SALWEN PAPER PRODUCTS
Brooklyn, New York
Commercial, Office Building
Completed: 1970s

SANG & POLLAK
Brooklyn, New York
Commercial, Office Building
Completed: 1970s

SARAH NEUMAN
845 Palmer Avenue
Mamaroneck, New York
Public/Institutional, Nursing Home

THE SARATOGA (pictured left)
330 East 75th Street
New York, New York
Market-Rate Residential Condominium
Completed: 1985

THE SAVANNAH
250 West 89th Street
New York, New York
Market-Rate Residential Condominium
Completed: 1986

SEA GATE COMMUNITY CENTER
Brooklyn, New York
Public/Institutional, Community
Completed: 1970s

SEATRAIN INTERNATIONAL
One Chase Manhattan Plaza
New York, New York
Commercial, Office Building
Completed: pre 1981

SEAVIEW MANOR
150 Brielle Avenue
Staten Island, New York
Senior Living
Completed: 1998

SELFHELP KISSENA APARTMENTS
42–25 Kissena Boulevard
Flushing, New York
Senior Living
Completed: 2002

SELIS MANOR
135 West 23rd Street
New York, New York
Affordable Housing, Assisted Living
Completed: 1980

SENECA BUFFALO CREEK CASINO
Buffalo, New York
Hospitality, Hotel

THE SEVILLE CONDOMINIUM
300 East 77th Street
New York, New York
Market-Rate Residential Condominium
Completed: 2000

SHAKESPEARE SENIOR HOUSING
1454 Shakespeare Avenue
Bronx, New York
Senior Living
Completed: 2003

THE SHERRY HOUSE
125 East 87th Street
New York, New York
Market-Rate Residential Rental
Completed: 1962

THE SIENA
188 East 76th Street
New York, New York
Market-Rate Residential Condominium
Completed: 1996

SILVERCREST SENIOR HOUSING
86–19 144th Street
Briarwood, New York
Senior Living
Completed: 2010

SIMON BOLIVAR APARTMENTS
981 Columbus Avenue
New York, New York
Adaptive Reuse, Conversion
Completed: late 1980s

SISTERS OF MERCY CONVENT
273 Willoughby Avenue
Brooklyn, New York
Adaptive Reuse, Rehabilitation
Completed: 1996

SKY CLUB
700 First Street
Hoboken, New Jersey
Market-Rate Residential Condominium
Completed: 2004

SKYLINE COMMONS
Parsons Boulevard, Goethals Avenue, and 82nd Drive
Jamaica, New York
Senior Living

SOBRO BROOK AVENUE RESIDENCE
Bronx, New York
Public/Institutional, Nursing Home

SOHO COURT
301 Elizabeth Street
New York, New York
Market-Rate Residential Rental
Completed: 1996

THE SOLAIRE (pictured p. 368)
20 River Terrace
New York, New York
Market-Rate Residential Rental
Completed: 2003

SOLARIA RIVERDALE
640 W 237th Street
Bronx, New York
Market-Rate Residential Condominium
Completed: 2008

SOLO-HORTON BRUSH COMPANY
New York, New York
Commercial, Office Building
Completed: 1970s

SONS AND DAUGHTERS OF MOSES
1160 Teller Avenue
Bronx, New York
Public/Institutional, Nursing Home

SOPHIAS HOUSE

542 West 153rd Street

New York, New York

Affordable Housing

SOUTH COVE PLAZA, BATTERY PARK CITY

50 Battery Place

New York, New York

Market-Rate Residential Rental

Completed: 1998

SPECTOR FREIGHT

Brooklyn, New York

Commercial, Office Building

Completed: 1970s

SR. LOUISE DEMARILLAC MANOR

9 Hygeia Place

Staten Island, New York

Affordable/Supportive Housing

Completed: 2012

The Solaire

ST. BARNABAS HOSPITAL

Bronx, New York

Healthcare

Completed: 1980s

ST. ELIZABETH'S MANOR

Brielle Avenue

Staten Island, New York

Senior Living, Assisted Living

ST. JOHN'S APARTMENTS

287 Prospect Avenue

Brooklyn, New York

Affordable Housing

Completed: 1998

ST. JOHN'S LAW SCHOOL

81–50D Utopia Parkway

Jamaica, New York

Adaptive Reuse, Recycled

Completed: 1970s

ST. JOHN'S UNIVERSITY

– Jamaica, New York

– Staten Island, New York

Public/Institutional, Education Facility

ST. JOSEPH BY THE SEA HIGH SCHOOL

Staten Island, New York

Public/Institutional, Education Facility

ST. LEONARD'S FAMILY HOUSING

60 Wilson Avenue

Brooklyn, New York

Affordable/Low-Income Housing

Completed: 2005

ST. LUKE'S/ROOSEVELT HOSPITAL

New York, New York

Public/Institutional, Hospital

ST. PAUL THE APOSTLE SENIOR HOUSING

55–06 99th Street

Corona, New York

Senior Living

Completed: 2002

ST. PIUS V

105–20 Liverpool Street

Jamaica, New York

Senior Living

Completed: 2000

ST. TERESA OF AVILA SENIOR HOUSING

549–535 St. Johns Place

Brooklyn, New York

Senior Living

Completed: 2004

ST. VINCENT DE PAUL

900 Intervale Avenue

Bronx, New York

Senior Living, Assisted Living, Conversion

Completed: 2012

STATEN ISLAND UNIVERSITY HOSPITAL HOUSING

Staten Island, New York

Healthcare

Completed: 1970s

STRATFORD HOUSE

1168–1172 Stratford Avenue

Bronx, New York

Adaptive Reuse, Rehabilitation

Completed: 2002

SYOSSET HOSPITAL

Syosset, New York

Public/Institutional, Hospital

Completed: 1970s

T BUILDING, QUEENS HOSPITAL

82–68 164th Street

Jamaica, New York

Affordable/Supportive Housing

TANYA TOWERS

620 East 13th Street

New York, New York

Residential

Completed: 1973

TAYSTEE

430 West 126th Street

New York, New York

Office Building

TECHNICAL INDUSTRIAL PARK

Plainview, New York

Commercial, Office Building

Completed: 1970s

TEMPLE BETHEL OF CEDARHURST

Cedarhurst, New York

Public/Institutional, Synagogue

TEMPLE EMANUEL – GREAT NECK

Great Neck, New York

Public/Institutional, Synagogue

TEMPLE EMANUEL – NEW HYDE PARK

New Hyde Park, New York

Public/Institutional, Synagogue

TEMPLE ISIAH

1 Chelsea Place

Great Neck, New York

Public/Institutional, Synagogue

TEMPLE ISRAEL

New York, New York

Public/Institutional, Synagogue

Completed: 1967

TEMPLE RODEPH SHOLOM

New York, New York

Public/Institutional, Synagogue

TEMPLE SHOLOM

Bellerose Floral Park

263-10 Union Turnpike

Glen Oaks, New York

Public/Institutional, Synagogue

TEMPLE SINAI

71–11 112th Street

Forest Hills, New York

Public/Institutional, Synagogue

Completed: 1963

THEATRE ROW

410 West 42nd Street

New York, New York

Commercial, Theater

TIFFANY & COMPANY

New York, New York

Commercial

Toyota of Manhattan

TINTON HOUSE SUPPORTIVE HOUSING

942–960 Tinton Avenue

Bronx, New York

Affordable/Supportive Housing

Completed: 2004

TOWER 49

12 East 49th Street

New York, New York

Commercial, Office Building

Completed: 1984

TOYOTA OF MANHATTAN

(pictured above)

645 11th Avenue

New York, New York

Commercial

TRAFALGAR HOSPITAL

161 East 90th Street

New York, New York

Healthcare

Completed: 1970s

TRANSPORTATION WORKERS UNION

Queens, New York

Affordable Housing

Completed: pre-1980s

TRAVIS SCHOOL

Cedarhurst, New York

Public/Institutional, Education Facility

Completed: 1970s

TRIANGLE (pictured p. 371)

43–12 Hunter Street

Long Island City, New York

Market-Rate Residential

TRINITY SCHOOL

New York, New York

Public/Institutional, Education Facility

TUXEDO PLACE

41 Hospital Road

Tuxedo, New York

Senior/Assisted Living

Completed: 2001

TWIN TOWER APARTMENTS

199 Yacht Street

Bridgeport, Connecticut

Residential

Completed: 1970s

TWO COLUMBUS PLACE

2 Columbus Avenue

New York, New York

Market-Rate Residential Condominium

Completed: 1998

UNITED ARTIST CINEMAS

New York, New York

Commercial, Cinema

UNITED SHOE MACHINERY

Brooklyn, New York

Commercial, Office Building

Completed: 1970s

UNITED STATES BRONZE

New Hyde Park, New York

Commercial, Office Building

Completed: 1970s

UNITED WIRE & METAL WORKERS UNION HEALTH CENTER

New York, New York

Public/Institutional, Hospital

Completed: 1970s

UNIVERSITY SENIOR HOUSING

1285 Merriam Avenue and
West 169th Street

Bronx, New York

Senior Living

Completed: 2007

UNIVERSITY SHOPPING CENTER

Canton, New York

Commercial, Retail/Shopping Center

Completed: pre-1981

URBAN GLASS HOUSE

330 Spring Street

New York, New York

Market-Rate Residential Condominium

Completed: 2005–2007

THE VANDEWATER

543 West 122nd Street

New York, New York

Market-Rate Residential Condominium

VETERANS AFFAIRS HOSPITAL

New York, New York

Healthcare

Completed: 1970s

THE VICTORY

561 Tenth Avenue

New York, New York

Market-Rate Residential Rental

Completed: 2001

THE VOGUE

990 Sixth Avenue

New York, New York

Market-Rate Residential Rental

Completed: 1987

WAGNER COLLEGE (SOLAR POWER)

Staten Island, New York

Public/Institutional, Education Facility

Completed: 1970s

WARING AVENUE

Bronx, New York

Public/Institutional, Healthcare

Completed: 1970s

WASHINGTON AVENUE APARTMENTS

1138 Washington Avenue

Bronx, New York

Affordable Housing

Completed: 2009

WASHINGTON SCHOOL APARTMENTS

New Rochelle, New York

Adaptive Reuse, Conversion

Completed: 1970s

Triangle

WAYNE HOUSING

Wayne, New Jersey

Affordable Housing

Completed: 1970s

THE WEDGEWOOD

499 North Broadway

White Plains, New York

Residential

Completed: 1966

WEILER HOSPITAL | CARDIAC CATH LAB #2

1825 Eastchester Road

Bronx, New York

Public/Institutional, Hospital

THE WEST BANK

359 West 11th Street

New York, New York

Market-Rate Residential Condominium

Completed: 1999

WESTCHESTER JEWISH CENTER

Mamaroneck, New York

Public/Institutional, Synagogue

Completed: 1968

WESTCHESTER TRIANGLE

871 Westchester Avenue,

890 Prospect Avenue

Bronx, New York

Affordable Housing, Community

Completed: 1999

WHITE PLAINS SENIOR HOUSING

23–29 Quarropas Street,

112–122 Court Street

White Plains, New York

WHITNEY HOUSE APARTMENTS

200 East 90th Street

New York, New York

Market-Rate Residential Condominium

Completed: 1982

WICKERSHAM HOSPITAL

133 East 58th Street

New York, New York

Healthcare

Completed: 1970s

WILLOUGHBY

Brooklyn, New York

Public/Instiutional, Healthcare

Completed: pre-1981

THE WIMBLEDON

200 East 82nd Street

New York, New York

Market-Rate Residential Rental

Completed: 1980

WOODHULL HOSPITAL EMERGENCY SUITE

760 Broadway

Brooklyn, New York

Public/Institutional, Hospital

YESHIVA TORAS EMES

Brooklyn, New York

Education Facility

Completed: pre-1981

YONKERS HOUSING AUTHORITY**

Advisors on the desegregation case which provided 200 units of affordable housing scattered on seven sites throughout the city.

Early 1990s

YORKVILLE MEDICAL CENTER

New York, New York

Public/Institutional, Hospital

Completed: 1970s

YOUNG ISRAEL OF HILCREST

169–07 Jewel Avenue

Flushing, New York

Public/Institutional, Synagogue

Footnotes

* Armenian Children's Rehabilitation Center. One of the firm's earliest international projects, this rehabilitation center was built in 1989, the year after a devastating earthquake in Armenia killed 55,000 people. Al Efron led the pro-bono design effort for children injured in the disaster, many of whom lost limbs. The 10,000-square-foot center included out-patient space for physical, psychological, recreational, and occupational therapy; it also provided facilities for making and fitting prostheses on-site.

** Yonkers Housing Authority. In 1988, Federal judge Leonard B. Sand ruled in *United States v. Yonkers*, mandating with a desegregation order that low-income housing for 200 units scattered on seven sites be provided. (HBO's *Show Me a Hero* is based on these events.) SLCE prepared the proposals under which the two- and three-bedroom townhouses were constructed. The housing was completed on time by the use of steel- and wood-framed factory-built units.

IMAGE CREDITS

Page	Credit
2, 8–9	DBOX; courtesy of Macklowe Properties
13	Alan Schindler
14, 15	Inessa Binenbaum
17	Edit Photographic
18	Courtesy of TF Cornerstone
22	Lifang Vision Technology Co., Ltd.; courtesy of ADCO Group
24–25	DBOX; Courtesy of Five Points Development, LLC
26, 27	DBOX; Courtesy of RFR Holdings LLC
28	Hayes Davidson; courtesy of Hines
29	Courtesy of Hines
30–31, 32, 33	Lifang Vision Technology Co., Ltd.; courtesy of Greystar Europe Holdings Limited
34	Inessa Binenbaum
35	Courtesy of World Wide Holdings
38, 39	Noe & Associates with the Boundary; courtesy of Bizzi & Partners Development LLC
40, 41, 42, 43	Robert A.M. Stern Architects; courtesy of Vornado Realty Trust
44	James Ewing and Robert A.M. Stern Architects; courtesy of Zeckendorf Development LLC
45	By-Encore; courtesy of Toll Brothers City Living
46	BINYAN Studios; courtesy of BLDG Management
47	TF Cornerstone
48–49	RSpline
50	Kohn Pedersen Fox Associates PC
52–53	Courtesy of Rockrose Development, LLC
56-57, 58	Redundant Pixel; courtesy of Rockrose Development, LLC
59	Courtesy of Rockrose Development, LLC
60, 61	quallsbenson; courtesy of Time Equities Inc.
62	Evan Joseph Images; courtesy of Property Markets Group
63	RSpline
64	Richard Berenholtz; courtesy of The Durst Organization
65	Iwan Baan; courtesy of The Durst Organization
66	Field Condition; courtesy of The Durst Organization
67 (T)	Iwan Baan; courtesy of The Durst Organization
67 (B)	Alex Fradkin; courtesy of The Durst Organization
68, 69	Alan Schindler
70	Archpartners; courtesy of Robert A.M. Stern Architects
71	Evan Joseph Images; courtesy of Extell Development Company
72, 73	Courtesy of Mega Contracting Group
74–75	Jeremy Frechette
76–79, 80	Inessa Binenbaum
81	Jacob Snavely; courtesy of JD Carlisle Development Corp.
82–83, 84–85	Courtesy of Gotham Organization
86–87	Courtesy of TF Cornerstone
88–89, 90, 91	DBOX; courtesy of Macklowe Properties and CIM Group
92	Courtesy of Zeckendorf Development LLC
93	Hayes Davidson
96–97	Corporate Photographics: Bob Zucker
98–99	Courtesy of LCOR
100 (T)	Tangram 3DS, Courtesy of AvalonBay Communities, Inc.
100 (B)	Courtesy of AvalonBay Communities, Inc.
101	RSpline
102, 103	Sylvester Zawadzki; courtesy of L+M Development Partners
104, 105 (B)	Inessa Binenbaum
106	DBOX
107	Tectonic Photo
108–109	Inessa Binenbaum
110–111	Evan Joseph Images; courtesy of Extell Development Company
112	Evan Joseph Images
113 (T)	Courtesy of Extell Development Company
113 (B)	Atelier Christian de Portzamparc
114–115	Hanna Browning
118–119, 120–121	Eastdil Photography; courtesy of Kenbar Management
122	Courtesy of Roseland Management
124–125	ARCHPHOTO; courtesy of Hines
126	Inessa Binenbaum
129	Jeff Goldberg/ESTO; courtesy of The Albanese Organization
130	Courtesy of LCOR
136	Inessa Binenbaum
139	Alan Schindler
140	John W. Cahill

142, 143	Courtesy of Zeckendorf Development LLC
144	Fetner
145, 147	Inessa Binenbaum
146	Peter Mauss/Esto
149	Corporate Photographics: Bob Zucker
152, 153	Courtesy of Continental Ventures
154–155, 156	Tectonic Photo
157	Courtesy of Hines
158	Inessa Binenbaum
158–159 (TR, BR)	Courtesy of Roseland Management
160–161	Inessa Binenbaum
162	Corporate Photographics: Bob Zucker
163	Courtesy of The Albanese Organization
164	Inessa Binenbaum
165, 166, 167	Courtesy of Roseland Management
168	Courtesy of World Wide Holdings
170	Inessa Binenbaum
170–171 (TL, BL)	Courtesy of Steinberg & Pokoik Management Corp.
172–173	Courtesy of Gotham Organization
181	Courtesy of The Albanese Organization
182	Corporate Photographics: Bob Zucker
184, 185	Tectonic Photo
187	Tectonic Photo; courtesy of Gotham Organization
194–195	Inessa Binenbaum
199	Tectonic Photo
200	James Ewing; courtesy of The Brodsky Organization
210	Hanna Browning
212, 213	Inessa Binenbaum
215	Courtesy of Monadnock Construction Inc.
216–217, 218, 219	Hanna Browning
220–221	Edit Photographic
223, 224, 225	Hanna Browning
226–227	Inessa Binenbaum
228, 229, 230	Hanna Browning
231	Courtesy of L+M Development Partners
232	Hanna Browning
239	Corporate Photographics: Bob Zucker
242	Alla Schechter
243, 244	Inessa Binenbaum
254, 255	Paul Rivera; courtesy of Vornado Realty Trust
256–257	Inessa Binenbaum
258, 259	Courtesy of Macklowe Properties
260, 261	Courtesy of 75 Wall Associates, LLC
262–263	Tectonic Photo
264, 265	Courtesy of The Albanese Organization
269	Tectonic Photo
278, 288–289	Corporate Photographics: Bob Zucker
280	Courtesy of Monadnock Construction, Inc.
304–305	Williams New York
306	Getty Images
307	Williams New York
310, 311	DBOX; courtesy of Civic Center Community Group Broadway LLC
312, 313	Courtesy of Macklowe Properties
314	Hanna Browning
315, 322, 323	Corporate Photographics: Bob Zucker
324, 325	Courtesy of World Wide Holdings
327	SLCE Architects
329 (L)	Corporate Photographics: Bob Zucker
330, 331	Courtesy of World Wide Holdings
336	Corporate Photographics: Bob Zucker
340	Evan Joseph Images
341	SLCE Architects
342	Noë & Associates and The Boundary
345, 346, 349	Hanna Browning
350	Courtesy of OKO Group
355	Courtesy of Gotham Organization
358	Evan Joseph Images; courtesy of Rose Associates
366	Courtesy of The Albanese Organization
370, 371	SLCE Architects

KEY

T	Top
B	Bottom
L	Left
TL	Top Left
TR	Top Right
BL	Bottom Left
BR	Bottom Right

ACKNOWLEDGMENTS

SLCE Architects owes its continuing success in no small part to the dedicated efforts of its clients, associates, and staff, and this book is a small way of saying thank you for the invaluable partnerships and collaborations we've formed over the last 77 years.

Special recognition is owed to Louise Allen, whose tireless and impeccably organized management of this project is the reason it moved forward.

— *Current Partners of SLCE*

SLCE PARTNERS AND CONTRIBUTING YEARS TO PARTNERSHIP

Sid Schuman, 1941–1984

Sam Lichtenstein, 1941–1991

Peter Claman, partner from 1973–2010

Al Efron, partner from 1977–1998

Jerrold Clarke, partner from 1988–2001

Enzo Depol, partner from 1988–2011

Saky Yakas, 1985–present (partner since 1996)

James Davidson, 1984–present (partner since 1996)

Luigi Russo, 1994–present (partner since 2002)

Robert Laudenschlager, 1997–present (partner since 2005)

Gloria Glas, 1985–present (partner since 2007)

Mario Yao, 1982–present (partner since 2011)

Paul Albano, 1994–present (partner since 2018)

CONTRIBUTORS

Saky Yakas

Writer and contributor

James Davidson

Writer and contributor

PUBLICATION ASSISTANTS

Louise Allen (lead)

Elizabeth Christian

Matthew Shufelt

Matthew Hampel

George Liao

Artifice Press Limited
298 Regents Park Road, London, N3 2SZ
United Kingdom

+44 (0)20 8371 4000
office@artificeonline.com
www.artificeonline.com

Designed by Artifice Press.

British Library in Cataloguing Data
A CIP record for this book is available from the British Library.

ISBN 978-1-911339-06-9

Printed in the UK by CPi Colour.

Artifice